MASTER JIU-JITSU MASTER LIFE

PAUL KINDZIA

HOW TO CREATE AN EXTRAORDINARY LIFE THROUGH JIU-JITSU

MASTER JIU-JITSU MASTER LIFE

KINDZIA

Master Jiu-Jitsu
Master Life

How To Create An Extraordinary Life Through Jiu-Jitsu

www.masterjiujitsumasterlife.com

ISBN-13: 978-0692161975
ISBN-10: 069216197X

Published by Paul Kindzia, Inc.

Printed in the United States of America

Cover Design – **Thomas McGee**

Editing – Jason Talley and Angela Kindzia

Cover Model - The most talented black belt hand model in all of jiu-jitsu – Tyler (Sweet T.) Driskell.

For other queries, contact:

questions@paulkindzia.com

For additional valuable information including free resources, please visit our website at:

www.masterjiujitsumasterlife.com

When you are exposed to the jiu-jitsu community, you will meet countless people that share a similar message which is, "Jiu-Jitsu has changed my life." What many people have discovered is the power of Jiu-Jitsu on and off the practice mats. Jiu-Jitsu can teach you, move you, provide you with new perspectives, and help shape you as a person. It could be one of the most powerful influences that will impact you for a lifetime. We teach proven tips, processes, and timeless principles through the practice of jiu-jitsu that results in happier, more fulfilling, and balanced lives. We laugh a lot too.

ACKNOWLEDGEMENTS

Thank you to my wife Angela who supported me on this incredible deep dive into Jiu-Jitsu. It is one thing to repeatedly state, proclaim, yell, shout, preach, and grandstand that the most important investments are in yourself, your body, and your health. It is another to walk the walk and arrange one's affairs to live that philosophy yourself day after day. It would be impossible to eat, sleep, train, rest, study, recharge, learn, work, read, observe, travel, consult, research, write, produce, and get through the days without the unending support that it takes to fuel the machine.

I would like to thank all the training partners that are such a positive influence on my journey. Thank you to all the academy owners that I visited for the extra personal support, coaching, and investment in my jiu-jitsu and leading through example.

Thank you to those instructors who are pushing jiu-jitsu forward, promoting safe training protocols, and for setting up the infrastructure and environment for the rest of us to benefit from and enjoy. Your academies and the atmospheres are the building blocks of changed lives. None of it would have been possible for any of us if you didn't pave the way and trailblaze for the rest of us. I am grateful.

Thank you to the organizations that are promoting the growth of jiu-jitsu across all age and genders worldwide and the incredible teams of people working to share the message and learning principles of jiu-jitsu. You have made such a positive impression on my jiu-jitsu experience.

Thank you to Ryan Ford from the Grappling Central Podcast, Byron Jabara from the BJJ Brick Podcast, Stephan Kesting from GrappleArts.com/Strenuous Life Podcast, and Andre Borges at the BJJ Heroes website (www.bjjheroes.com) There are many people in the jiu-jitsu community such as these excellent examples that have worked enormous hours and put in endless efforts for the benefit of others (for years). I am grateful for their tireless contributions to the community and selfless acts of generosity sharing their time and talents. You have made such a positive impact on my life, and I appreciate you.

Thank you to all the academy owners who are striving to change lives through teaching jiu-jitsu. Academy owners are usually not individuals who are searching for great fame or fortune in their endeavors. They have all generously established churches for lost souls who need a place to call home. A place for people to make friends. A place for people to self-reflect and make changes to themselves. A place to help them figure out life.

PROLOGUE

Before you begin your journey through the book, I encourage you to keep things in perspective, relax, and enjoy the read or listen if consuming via audiobook. You will come across plenty of names. You may be familiar with some of the names and not familiar with many of the names. There is no test at the end of the book. There is no need to memorize names or academies. Their stories are meant to educate and inspire you.

You will find that many members of the Gracie family are mentioned in this book. Although this book is not a history of Gracie Jiu-Jitsu (that would be an entire book in and of itself), there are a few important takeaways that are important for you to understand as you proceed along your jiu-jitsu journey and make your way through this book.

The Gracie family could and should be considered the royal family of jiu-jitsu. They did not invent jiu-jitsu, but their influence over the art was significant enough to form a style of their own. Whether you call that Gracie Jiu-Jitsu or Brazilian Jiu-Jitsu, without the Gracie family and many of its specific members, it's hard to imagine how the sport would have expanded around the globe as it has.

You should know that Carlos Gracie (Sr.) and Helio Gracie were from a large family that included five brothers and were born in the early 1900's. These men were passionate enough about martial arts that they began integrating and innovating techniques that originated from Judo, Japanese Jiu-Jitsu and other martial arts. They focused their area of expertise on ground fighting which neutralized the advantages normally held by a bigger or stronger opponent. This laid the foundation for what we are enjoying today in jiu-jitsu.

Carlos Sr. and Helio would each go on to have very large families of their own and these expansive families produced various children, grandchildren, nieces, nephews and cousins that were very active in the family passion of jiu-jitsu. These second and third generations (and beyond) of Gracie's also contributed greatly to the expansion of the art.

The Gracie's style of jiu-jitsu proved to be extremely effective in real world application. Beyond technical innovation in the martial arts, the Gracie family members were instrumental in several areas that were critical in the growth and expansion of the art through the 20th century. The Gracie's were excellent promoters of seminars, challenge matches, exhibitions, marketing, organizing tournaments, and creating what would become a network of schools specific to teaching jiu-jitsu to students. They also were instrumental in the successful efforts to bring jiu-jitsu into communities all around the world.

We are all connected and highly influenced as practitioners in some way, shape, or form through the lineage of Gracie Jiu-Jitsu. In many ways, we are all members of one global jiu-jitsu family. Now onward to your journey.

FROM THE AUTHOR

Several years ago, I found myself wanting some new experiences in my life. Things were getting stale, repetitive in a not so good way, and all too familiar. I was also looking for a new writing project and considered a variety of topics.

I was always curious about the martial arts going back to my teenage years and this continued as a young adult. In fact, while living with my parents during a stretch in college, I asked my mother if I could buy this thing called a Pay-Per-View from our local cable provider so that I could watch the very first Ultimate Fighting Championship (UFC 1). I taped the event using the revolutionary technology called a VHS tape on a Video Cassette Recorder (VCR).

UFC 1 had a Pay-Per-View buyrate of 86,000 along with a live gate of 7,800 on that fateful day of November 12, 1993. I still remember watching Royce Gracie win the tournament using something called jiu-jitsu against much larger and more physically dominant opponents. I became a fan of the UFC and continued to be intrigued by jiu-jitsu. Over the next two decades, I just assumed that the activity of jiu-jitsu was something that combat athletes did to become better fighters, not something that normal people did as physical and mental exercises.

Now, a few decades older, I tip-toed with trepidation into a local jiu-jitsu academy, still not fully committed to the physical endeavor nor what would become a large writing project. I went in with the approach that I would be a fly on the wall, an observer, a participating journalist getting in some exercise and becoming more familiar with what I was watching on TV as a fan. I could get some exercise, learn some new things, and document the experience for myself and see where things went.

I quickly noticed a few things that surprised me. First, I noticed how many "normal" people were practicing the art of jiu-jitsu. There were kids, men, and women, that were young and old. There were people that went to church on Sunday's, people with corporate jobs, doctors that worked at hospitals, and many people that were shy and introverted. I am not a shy or introverted guy but had high levels of anxiety and fear at the start of my jiu-jitsu journey. I cannot even believe the courage that these others would need to muster to show up to practice and walk through the front door of the academy. It was impressive and inspiring.

The second thing that struck me as surprising is how often I heard the phrase, "Jiu-Jitsu changed my life." I'll admit, after a few times hearing this I would often roll my eyes and internally snicker. "How could so many people say that jiu-jitsu changed their lives? It is just ridiculous."

However, as the months of jiu-jitsu training continued which then turned into years, two things happened in my own life. First, I fell in love with jiu-jitsu. I should state the more accurate statement which is I fanatically fell in love with jiu-jitsu. Second, I caught myself repeatedly saying to myself and then to others, "Jiu-jitsu changed my life."

How could this be? What changed? Why did these changes occur? How does jiu-jitsu change a person's life? The big reasons were obvious. I got in incredible shape as I trained consistently. I was stronger, flexible, moved better, and my coordination improved. I lost weight. I made friends, lots of friends. I started competing and had an outlet to scratch that competitive itch that seems to follow me around. I learned some self-defense techniques which made me feel more confident in myself. No person wants to walk the earth constantly feeling physically vulnerable to the aggressive whims of others.

However, what was more important than these wonderful benefits of jiu-jitsu, was that I noticed that my entire life started changing for the better. It was like I was operating on an entirely elevated level. "Why? Why was my life getting better through jiu-jitsu?" The reasons were not clear in the beginning.

As I continued my training, I searched for ways to expedite my learning process in jiu-jitsu. It is a very hard activity to become proficient in. It is a challenge, to say the least. I began studying others; legends of the sport, icons, innovators, influencers, and world-class champions.

Many of these individuals used different styles of jiu-jitsu, different strategies, and varying techniques. Trying to learn all of them proved to be ineffective and inefficient. There was something more though. There had to be some commonalities between them. There had to be common denominators of success. "What were those common denominators?" I asked myself.

Then it struck me. There were common denominators of success between these individuals who were successful. They used similar principles in their life. They were using life principles in jiu-jitsu and jiu-jitsu principles in life with impressive results. I pointed my focus in that direction and started paying attention to these principles and how I could apply them in my journey through jiu-jitsu.

That is how jiu-jitsu changed my life. That is why my life is so much better now than it was before jiu-jitsu. I have so much more clarity. I have so many more tools. I have a better roadmap to personal success.

The jiu-jitsu history lesson that I received along the way was just a giant bonus for which I am grateful. Many instructors themselves are forgetting a major fact and reality of modern day jiu-jitsu. As kids and young adults enter the world of jiu-jitsu, they have no idea of the history of jiu-jitsu. They do not have any idea who the Gracie's are, or how Royce Gracie used jiu-jitsu to defeat larger and stronger fighters in UFC 1 in 1993. Many were not even born in 1993. They did not watch UFC 1 like many jiu-jitsu blackbelts today.

This book is a combination of a little bit of important history of jiu-jitsu, the stories of legends and icons, but more importantly the story of how jiu-jitsu can help you master your life if you pay attention to what we can learn through others before us.

I hope you will one day say the same thing as so many of the others, including myself which is, "Jiu-jitsu changed my life."

Peace, Love, and Jiu-Jitsu!
Paul

TABLE OF CONTENTS

Introduction

"One can have no smaller or greater mastery than mastery of oneself" – Leonardo da Vinci

For those that practice the art, they say that jiu-jitsu is a portal to an alternative life. It is a gateway for those that want to walk through a different door into the vast universe of wonderment. The choice of practicing the art is the red door in personal Feng Shui that can lead to better health, more confidence, strong social relationships, and a path towards personal transformation and self-improvement. Jiu-jitsu is even more than that. Jiu-jitsu is a course-curriculum in the skills needed to win at life.

Most people stumble and bounce through life bumbling, fumbling, and crashing from one obstacle to another. You were encouraged to follow a misguided educational system and were expected to obey the mainstream concepts that were in vogue at the time, usually at the expense of any valuable learning that results in a fulfilling life. You were taught to meet minimum standards set by self-empowering institutions as you made your way through grade school memorizing facts, names, and skewed historical perspectives.

You were taught to fit in, be like everybody else, and consume what culture is serving up in attempts to fill the voids in your life with immediate gratification. You search for answers to take your mind off the fact that you have no real idea what you are doing in life, where you are going, where you want to go, or how to get there even if you did. You try and make your way like everybody around you navigating credit card debt, failed relationships, unfulfilling jobs, waning health, and kid's soccer games.

What if you are learning the wrong things in life? What if you are learning in the wrong ways? What if you are chasing the wrong things? What if everything you need to lead a fulfilling life is right there in front of you, but you just never noticed? What if the key to unleashing your human potential is not the pursuit of fame, or fortune, or pleasure, but rather the pursuit of mastery? Moreover, what if, ironically enough, it is through the pursuit and accomplishment of mastery one often finds themselves with the desired results which could include the fame, the fortune, and the pleasures of achievement?

A Young Man Chooses Mastery As The Path

Espen Mathiesen is not a large man. He looks to be more like a boy trying to find his way out of the youth cocoon and into manhood. He has an innocent young face with light colored hair typical of those of Scandinavian decent. Mathiesen was born and raised in Egersund, a small town on the west coast of Norway that is similar to others around it. These small towns littering the coastal communities rely on the bounties of the oceans and waterways encapsulating the communities. The locals are hearty seamen, fisherman, and are weathered to withstand the harsh elements of nature.

Norwegians are well known for their love of winter sports; skiing, ice skating, and anything else that mixes in the opportunity to push oneself in an environment that would make a polar bear put on a hat before playing. Mathiesen was like most of the other Norwegian children, playing the usual winter sports during the long winters, and football (American soccer) in the summer. However, by the age of 15 Mathiesen would already be confronting some inner conflicts that were brewing in the young lad who was supposed to play football, study his math and physics so he could become an engineer, and go on to pursue a degree at a university.

How many times have you heard of a story of a boy who is supposed to live life by the norms of the local cultures and society, yet has a yearning to go in a completely different direction against the better advice of just about everybody around them? Mathiesen had an internal problem, a big one, and was struggling with how to reconcile this issue in his Norwegian existence. By the age of 16, only one year after being officially exposed to the art of jiu-jitsu, he knew that he had fallen in love with the endeavor.

Mathiesen had taken advantage of an opportunity to train with a local blue belt who besides being a doctor, was teaching jiu-jitsu three times a week to anybody and everybody who could be persuaded to step onto the mats for practice. Seven months later and Mathiesen was "all-in" mentally and emotionally. He would quit playing football so that he could have more time outside of school to focus on jiu-jitsu. Roadblocks started to appear, and it was obvious Mathiesen needed a new plan and quickly. He was barely 16 years old when his instructor would relocate and move away.

The self-reliant Mathiesen decided to team up with a local neighbor and friend who also had an interest in jiu-jitsu. The two of them made a financial investment and purchased some grappling mats. Soon enough the dynamic duo found themselves training several hours a day, six days a week. Mathiesen assembled his learning curriculum based on internet videos and instructional videos, and then studied and drilled the techniques until he felt he was proficient in them.

At the age of 17, Mathiesen traveled to Brazil under the tutelage of Jose Carlos at the Kimura Novo União headquarters. He now had the opportunity to test his skills against the highest caliber of practitioners. These were men and women who lived on the mats and were born with jiu-jitsu blood flowing through their veins. After six weeks of training in Brazil, Mathiesen returned to Norway with the growing inner conflict that was building in amplitude like a volcano ready to erupt.

How does one tell the locals, or friends, or parents that they want to dedicate their life to the art of jiu-jitsu? The responses must have included the predictable ones such as, "What is jiu-jitsu? Oh, is that like karate or Tae Kwon Do?" How could this major life decision be taken as sane or reasonable by anybody who is normal and most likely doesn't have any familiarity with the art?

Mathiesen was not living in Southern California, São Paulo, Brazil, or anywhere close to any mainstream jiu-jitsu communities scattered around the world. To say that jiu-jitsu in Norway is a fringe activity is an enormous understatement. Here is this good-looking great student who is well-read, ambitious, and with unlimited academic and professional potential in front of him and he wants to do jiu-jitsu? That makes no sense. Unless of course, you are Espen Mathiesen.

Mathiesen ended up having some much-needed ammunition to fight his fight and balance the forces of societal pressure and his struggle from within. He continued entering jiu-jitsu competitions and winning matches. By the spring of 2014, he won the European Championships as a blue belt which led to his promotion to purple belt by March of that same year. It is easier to squash the naysayers when one is winning and showing talent and skills, no matter the outlet. Perhaps the boy was onto something unique and special?

Now at the tender age of 18, the stars started to align, and the force was behind him in his quest for self-discovery. Mathiesen would arrange to travel to the United States in the summer of 2014 as a 19-year-old to visit California to train with the legendary Mendes Brothers and then to Arizona to train with highly regarded coach Gustavo Dantas.

In 2015, as a purple belt, the 20-year-old Mathiesen won the silver medal in the World Championships. In 2016 he moved to Haugesund to join forces with two other Norwegian standouts, Tommy Langaker and Vegard Randeberg. As a 21-year-old brown belt, Mathiesen won the prestigious IBJJF Pan American and European titles and was promoted to black belt by José Carlos in 2017 at the tender age of 22.

Mathiesen's journey is a remarkable story on so many different levels. How could this story even happen? How could a young Norwegian boy with no real access to top level academies or training partners most of the year become one of the most talented grapplers on the planet in his early 20's? How did the boy figure out the path to his dreams and navigate the treacherous cultural waters around him? How could a normal Scandinavian boy transform himself like this in such a compressed amount of time?

What you will discover is that without knowing exactly how to define it for himself or realizing it from an academic or behavioral perspective, the young Mathiesen was pursuing mastery the entire time. Mathiesen intuitively figured out the path to mastery and put himself on that path using the proven principles of success.

The Science Of Learning

Some saw Mathiesen's situation as a limiter. He did not have top notch training facilities, elite world class training partners, a high variety of training partners, or a championship team infrastructure around him. Nor did he have any direct role models in his local community that could serve as a template towards goal achievement. Mathiesen had to figure things out on his own, and it was because of this fact, along with his intelligence, instinct, and willingness to read and learn from sources outside of jiu-jitsu that he was able to leap ahead of thousands upon thousands of other practitioners.

Mathiesen was a student of more than jiu-jitsu. He was a student of cognitive psychology, learning, and many other disciplines. These behaviors are quite unusual for anyone in their late teenage years or early 20's. Mathiesen was reading books authored by Dr. Joe Dispenza such as "You Are The Placebo: Making Your Mind Matter" and "Becoming Supernatural: How Common People Are Doing The Uncommon." These are not easy books to read, let alone implement into one's life at any age.

Another book that made a huge impact on the young Mathiesen was "Make It Stick – The Science of Successful Learning" by Peter Brown, Henry Roediger III, and Mark McDaniel. "Make It Stick" was groundbreaking work on the science of learning as it showed how many common study habits and practice routines turn out to be counterproductive. Memorization, which is often emphasized in traditional education to pass a test, only creates the illusion of mastery, but those gains fade quickly. As the book explains, "More complex and durable learning comes from self-testing, introducing certain difficulties in practice, waiting to restudy new material until a little forgetting has set in, and interweaving the practice of one skill or topic with another."

The fact that Mathiesen was left to his own accord to learn jiu-jitsu early in his career without traditional instruction rooted in dogma allowed him to implement a self-developed curriculum based on scientific principles that were far more efficient in obtaining real mastery. Mathiesen wrote out training plans for half-year increments which were broken down into categories and sub-categories. One week he trained half-guard, followed by X-guard or some other position, which would lead to another position the third week. Mathiesen layed out the positions so that they all connected to the previous one based on how a roll or match would naturally evolve.

More importantly, Mathiesen was implementing proven principles of success that applied not just to jiu-jitsu, but to life itself that he could use in a variety of applications. Mathiesen was building his life and his daily habits around principles, not randomness. Principles such as consistency, discipline, processes, adaptability, minimalization, tracking, modelling, visualization, and habit are just some of the proven principles of mastery that the young Mathiesen would learn and implement into his own life.

The fact that Mathiesen would apply these principles to jiu-jitsu is secondary to his discovery of them so early in life that is so impressive. Most individuals will be born, live their entire lives, and never come close to learning and implementing these principles. As a result of this lack of knowledge and skillset, they will fall far short of their human potential.

In Mathiesen's case, he was not just becoming a black belt in jiu-jitsu. He was becoming a black belt in life. With his skills, he could be successful in whatever he chooses to apply himself in now that he had the building blocks of success. That is the beauty of jiu-jitsu if you pay attention. It will allow you the opportunity to learn the principles of success that could be applied to life itself so that your entire life is better and more productive.

Ideally, in addition to becoming a black belt in jiu-jitsu, you want to become a black belt in life through the pursuit of mastery. Become a black belt in health and wellness. Become a black belt on money and finance. Become a black belt in relationships. These are all possible as you navigate life with the proper principles of success and a mindset that should be pointed towards true mastery.

There is one central theme that you will encounter in jiu-jitsu and life along your road to mastery. It deals with quitting. You will see this quote later in the book, but the quote sets the tone for so much of what you will have to endure and thus it is worth repeating a few times.

"Jiu-jitsu exists to make you quit" – Paulo Ribeiro (fourth degree jiu-jitsu black belt)

Jiu-jitsu is a filter of life itself. Jiu-jitsu does not weed out people who are weak or lack coordination, or natural talent. Jiu-jitsu weeds out those who lack core principles of success. In jiu-jitsu, those that practice become stronger. Those that practice become more proficient. Those that practice eventually achieve mastery. To win, you must keep showing up and evolve as a person. However, that is the magic filter of jiu-jitsu, it weeds out those who are quitters. If you quit, there will be no self-mastery.

Mastery is not about holding the gold medal on the podium. Mastery is about losing the excess weight around your midsection, being mentally sharp, building strong bonds with others, learning how to learn, over-coming fears, and constantly learning new skills. It is the process of achieving what you may believe is unattainable with your life.

Mastery is about putting your whole heart into being the best at what you do and doing the things that you want to do. It is not about impressing your neighbors with a new car or being a great slave to your boss who wants his annual bonus to be a doozy. Mastery is about expressing yourself as an individual artist during your limited time on earth. For some, that may mean expressing themselves through painting, or playing the guitar, taking a photograph, cooking an original recipe, or in your case, practicing jiu-jitsu.

You have decided on a different form of self-expression, art, and pursuit of mastery through jiu-jitsu. It will change you as a person. It will make you better. It will make you stronger. It will change you at your core. Thousands of people have discovered the life changing benefits of jiu-jitsu and have gone on to lead incredible lives. At the same time, for all the known benefits of jiu-jitsu and the life transformational effects, the reality is, people will still quit jiu-jitsu no different than they will quit on their diet, quit on their workout program, quit school, quit on their relationships, or quit on anything that is hard but yields personal improvement.

Mastery of jiu-jitsu and self-mastery in life can flow in either direction. Such is the reality and truth in most endeavors. Once you develop, learn, and implement the principles of success in your life, you can apply them in various areas of life. Learning to learn is thus a critical component of success. The benefits of learning mastery have been known for centuries. In the year 1645, Japanese master swordsman Miymoto Musashi wrote, "If you know the way broadly, you will see it in everything." Alternatively, put another way, "If you know the way in one thing, you know the way in all things." The wisdom stems from his timeless book, "Go Rin No Sho (The Book of Five Rings) which to this day is a classic study on combat strategy, tactics, and philosophy.

If you learn what matters in the pursuit of success and achievement, you can apply it to jiu-jitsu and all areas of your life. These are the reasons why jiu-jitsu has resulted in so many personal transformations for practitioners. Long-term practitioners have been handed the keys to the library of success. Once they entered the knowledge vault, they only needed to read and study to become enlightened and enriched.

Do not be misled. You will suffer along the way. You will have failures and set-backs. You will have to learn to overcome these failures. However, it is this process of personal improvement that will transform you as an individual. Happiness will not come from avoiding the difficulties of life. Rather, it is the personal transformation that occurs during your journey that will provide meaning and fulfillment. It is when you find meaning in your life that you will find lasting happiness. May you find meaning through your practice of jiu-jitsu.

Principle 1: Mindset

"All of these people had character. None of them thought they were special people, born with the right to win. They were people who worked hard, who learned how to keep their focus under pressure, and who stretched beyond their ordinary abilities when they had to." – Carol Dweck, PhD

In 2012, Rob Kahn began speaking passionately to a large group of people that packed the mats at Gracie Tampa Jiu-Jitsu Academy, a school that Kahn founded many years earlier. Kahn isn't a tall man, but the thickness through his shoulders, arms, and chest on a human body that is built more like a community fire hydrant would still make a normal person say to themselves, "I'm not sure I want to mess around with this one." There is an unspoken demeanor to Kahn which gives you the sense that he likes to laugh but he would just as much rather smash your head and then laugh at a joke.

Kahn is no ordinary jiu-jitsu practitioner or instructor. Kahn began training in the mid 1990's and eventually under legendary three-time UFC champion Royce Gracie. He was a member of Royce Gracie's first group of black belts. Actually, he was Royce Gracie's first black belt to be fair and accurate. He is as close as you could get to the direct lineage of the family that is considered royalty amongst global practitioners without having Gracie blood and DNA running through his veins and anatomy himself.

It was Royce Gracie that put MMA on the map in UFC 1 when the Ultimate Fighting Championship was just a burgeoning experiment in the martial arts and sports entertainment world. Originally deemed a freak show and hated by regulators due to the lack of athlete protective rules, the early UFC events were a promotional attempt to finally solve the question, "What is the most effective martial art in a real fight?" Two combatants were locked inside a cage and allowed to use any and all martial arts techniques that they desired; karate, judo, sumo wrestling, kickboxing, and of course jiu-jitsu which at the time was relatively foreign and unfamiliar to most fans and competitors alike. The few rules that were in place were along the lines of, "No gouging the eyes, no grabbing another man's tic-tac's, etc." It was as close as you could get to, "The rules are, there are no rules."

It was at UFC 1 where the world was introduced to the real effectiveness of jiu-jitsu inside a cage, and it was none other than Royce Gracie, a slender non-athletic looking competitor in a plain white Gi that would change mixed martial arts forever. Royce, a Brazilian, was a blood member of the Gracie family, which is the royal family of jiu-jitsu. Royce would go on to win multiple championships in the UFC beating guys that appeared three times his size and doing it with what appeared to be ease.

This was the fuse that lit the dynamite in the global realm of jiu-jitsu as an effective and superior martial art.

Kahn, an American, was different than most practitioners in those early days. Not only was he a very early adaptor and practitioner of the Brazilian form of Gracie Jiu-Jitsu, but he was an early innovator in the sport. Kahn was interested in systematizing jiu-jitsu for the application in mixed martial arts and no-gi submission grappling rather than the traditional Gi style competitions which were the standard at the time and more consistent with the Brazilian practice of the art.

It was the creativity and experimentation that would allow Kahn to produce multiple UFC fighters and Abu Dhabi competitors. In addition to teaching professional fighters, Kahn passed these homegrown systems and knowledge through combative courses offered to Navy Seals, Army Rangers, other military special forces, and a host of additional law enforcement agencies. Kahn proved to be an effective early pioneer, even if unknown to most practitioners in an ever-growing fighting ecosystem.

Kahn wasn't a set-in-stone follower of all the traditions at the time but rather someone who pushed the envelope, tested techniques, and adapted specific strategies to what worked in real world fighting. He knew that for all the mysticism and cult like secrets proposed by martial arts and delivered to mesmerized self-defense practitioners, all that goes out the window once somebody gets punched in the face or is being choked out.

But on this day, Kahn was conducting a black belt promotional ceremony for one of his high performing students, Cris Rodriguez. Kahn described Rodriguez as his right hand, his left hand, his best friend, and then went on to describe the work ethic, ability, and perseverance that led up to this sentimental and emotional moment in time. Words such as "amazing" and "technical" were used with conviction during the ceremony and anyone that knew Rodriguez would agree in no uncertain terms.

Rodriguez started training martial arts at the age of 8 first taking up Tae Kwon Do and later beginning jiu-jitsu at the age of 15. Years and years of commitment to being what is often referred to in training circles as a "mat-rat" led to both a career in combat sports and as a highly effective instructor.

What made Rodriguez a bit different than the norm were a few things; first, Cris Rodriguez was a female in an incredibly male dominated sport and industry. Second, Rodriguez had a unique mind for learning that was cultivated over her lifetime. She had a passion for learning and took that passion deeper and with more commitment than the average person that puts on a jiu-jitsu gi.

Rodriguez claims she knew by the age of 11 that dedicating herself to a life of martial arts is what she wanted to do. By age 15 she was teaching Tae Kwon Do classes at a local academy to younger kids. By 16 she was the first female head instructor in the schools 30-year history.

Rodriguez practiced what she preached and was constantly passing on noble gems to her students. She reminded them that they can do anything that they can put their mind to and that everyday each of us make small decisions that lead up to something much greater than we realize at that time. Success is a result of those small day to day decisions that you won't even notice at any given moment, but when added up, the results are incredibly profound.

Rodriguez is everything that jiu-jitsu embodies; a demonstration of how a smaller opponent can win against a larger or stronger opponent by using technique, problem solving, and leverage. Rodriguez is only 5'2" and quickly became known as a terrifying opponent, even earning the nickname "Midget Twister" after modifying a jiu-jitsu technique known as "the twister" to adapt it to her smaller physical stature and frame.

She still had all the components for a long struggle with never ending problems and obstacles. She was a female in a male dominated activity in a fringe sport that is relatively unknown. She was a person who was small, physically weaker, and lacking the athleticism of most of her male training partners. One can only imagine that internally she had to endure some periodic and frequent episodes of doubt, but that someway and somehow the experience was going to all work out in a life plan for herself. Have you ever felt like you were never going to be able to overcome your personal limitations no matter how hard you try at something? If so, you know how Rodriguez must have felt many times during her youth.

Fortunately, when God made Rodriguez, the recipe called for 1 cup of tornado, a ½ cup of devil, and 2 scoops of intellectual bookworm. She was no ordinary combat athlete.

Rodriguez, the first American female blackbelt under the Gracie lineage, owns Gracie PAC which stands for "Parents and Children." The academy grew into a very large training and learning facility encompassing mat space and classrooms for children in the after-school programs. Whereas plenty of people teach jiu-jitsu, Rodriguez "is" jiu-jitsu and has since turned her skills into several lucrative businesses including an online learning resource called Jitz University for other owners of martial arts academies to effectively build and teach kids programs. Her curriculum and businesses are built upon the foundations of what can be referred to as "mindset."

Everything the school embodies is built from the foundation of mindset, something that Rodriguez has engrained in her personal pursuit of excellence and what she passionately instills in every one of her students.

The Research Behind The Importance of Mindset

When many practitioners think of the word "mindset" in jiu-jitsu, they often confuse it with the word "confidence," or the word "belief," whereby a competitor will harness their internal energy and focus on defeating a bigger or stronger opponent. They can compare it to sporting events or situations that were epic David and Goliath matchups that every fan relishes and archives in their memory in the category of what is possible.

But this isn't the mindset that is most critical to jiu-jitsu, business, or life. The term "mindset" refers to the belief that impacts one's ability to fulfill their personal potential. The use of the term "mindset" in this regard stems from the groundbreaking research and eventual best-selling book called "Mindset," by Carol Dweck, a Ph.D., and professor at Columbia University.

Dweck concluded after endless research of individuals of varying success that one's eventual accomplishments are based upon whether a person believes that their personal traits and abilities are fixed (and thus called a "fixed" mindset), or if they believe that traits and abilities are things that they could improve upon and develop, (and thus called a "growth" mindset).

Per Dweck's groundbreaking research, what prevents you from reaching your potential grows out of your mindset and biases towards your ability to learn, grow, and change yourself.   This insight allowed her to study, assess, and understand the common denominators of success of the greats in various activities such as music, sports, science, math, and business as well as understand why so many who appeared to have talent failed to reach their potential.

What is now clear and backed up by the sciences is that human qualities and abilities are not carved in stone. They are not fixed. These qualities and abilities simply yield to further influences such as work, effort, practice, study, and repetition. Humans are pliable beings because they are capable of learning, which means they can change, which means they are capable of growing.

If there is something that an academic jiu-jitsu blackbelt like Rodriguez has learned along her journey is that education and practice can bring about fundamental changes within us both physically and mentally. Jiu-jitsu is not an easy martial art to master. It's far from it.   It takes enormous amounts of practice, training, and learning. Just like any other endeavor, not all students learn the same way.   Practitioners start at different places, ages, and abilities. Eventual expertise in the art results from purposeful engagement during practice. It's not always the students that start out the most athletic or the strongest that end up the most proficient. It comes down to their pursuit of lifelong learning.

Rodriguez's success in the sport, business, and teaching is hinged on this concept of mindset. Learning is the fundamental ingredient to growth, and thus education is a pillar to that personal progress for any practitioner. Rodriguez values the education side of personal progress and comes armed with a degree in elementary education from the University of South Florida. She loves teaching, and the mats are her classroom to teach kids of all ages as well as adults.

For a female combat athlete to own and operate Tampa's largest martial arts academy, with hundreds of students is an impressive feat. At the core of her teachings is the belief that your future jiu-jitsu abilities and talents are not carved into stone at the start of your journey. Thinking that natural talent will deliver you to the promised land is simply a fixed mindset in action.

Fixed mindsets tend to believe that success comes down to natural talent or intelligence and that talent or intelligence is allocated out to each of us in life. The fixed mindset belief is that you either have it, or you don't have it. Believing that you have natural talent in an endeavor compels those with a fixed mindset to prove themselves repeatedly. If your talent is fixed, then you feel you need to keep demonstrating that talent to yourself and others to feel good about yourself.

Thus, jiu-jitsu practitioners that have a fixed mindset are more interested in looking smart or displaying natural talents that they were told they have (or believe they have) and to not look dumb or fail. Their journey has less to do with personal development and learning and more about not failing or looking stupid.

The very best jiu-jitsu practitioners have a growth mindset, not a fixed mindset. The growth mindset is one where you believe the hand you were dealt with is not the one you will be stuck with in the future. Many of the jiu-jitsu greats such as Caio Terra or Keenan Cornelius were far from natural freakish jiu-jitsu talents at the start of their jiu-jitsu pursuits. Rather, the hand they were dealt with was merely the starting point of their personal development. They believed and proved to themselves and others that their jiu-jitsu qualities were something that could be cultivated through additional efforts and practice. They, like everyone else, were able to change and grow through application and experience.

What is important to realize is that a person's true potential in jiu-jitsu and in life is unknown and unknowable at the start of their journeys because it is impossible to forecast what you can accomplish with years of passion, training, and learning. But keep one thing in mind front and center, if you believe that qualities can be developed (a growth mindset), then it is much more likely that you will develop a passion for learning and it is through this passionate learning that you will evolve as a practitioner in the art.

Those with a fixed mindset are more interested in wasting time repeatedly proving how great they are on the mats rather than getting better through practice and failure. They hide their deficiencies rather than overcoming them. The best practitioners stretch themselves, even when it isn't going well, which allows them to thrive during the constant challenging experiences that jiu-jitsu delivers to them.

Once you believe that you can develop, you begin to open yourself up to accurate feedback about your current abilities, even if that feedback is unflattering or deflating at times. If you focus on the learning, you will use that feedback to your advantage and grow through those opportunities.

A fixed mindset does the opposite. Those with a fixed mindset are concerned with how they will be judged in the immediate sense. Those with a fixed mindset are less focused on learning and improving and more focused on proving how talented they are. You can tell a practitioner with a fixed mindset on the practice mats because they are focused on "winning" in training and proving themselves against teammates. Rather than working on new techniques, or experimenting with less familiar positions, they stick to a few things that they feel the safest with repeatedly. They would rather "not lose" than practice at improving technique. This behavior eventually stunts their growth in the art and limits their potential.

The liability of a fixed mindset in jiu-jitsu, in business, and in life is that you are afraid of not being strong, or dominant, or talented. You end up rejecting the opportunities to learn. Those in a growth mindset are more interested in stretching themselves, challenging themselves, and developing more expertise.

Talent on and off the mats is something that must be worked for and earned, it isn't given to everybody. How many times have you seen people offered a challenge to learn on the mats by rolling with a more experienced and skilled opponent, but they pass up on it or are not interested due to their fixed mindset? But if you believe that success is about learning and growing, those with a growth mindset will seize the opportunity in training and competing. Fixed mindsets don't want to expose their deficiencies. That's how a fixed mindset eventually evolves people into non-learners.

High level jiu-jitsu practitioners never allow failure from practice (getting tapped out) to define their identity (believing that they personally are a failure). You must be careful of the fallacy that you either are born with jiu-jitsu talent, or you weren't. Many believe that you either have a natural ability in an endeavor or instead must expend all kinds of effort to develop that ability. The belief is that if one must expend effort and work hard, then they must not be great at it. It's also a belief that things must come easily to those who are true geniuses in the art. But the underlying reality is that those who have the work ethic and perseverance to keep learning, training, and growing make it all the way to the top and don't fall short of their potential.

Following the lessons of Rodriguez and the research of Dweck helps ensure that you don't take up a fixed mindset with your pursuit of jiu-jitsu or in other areas of your life. It takes the focus off the immediate outcome of your training. If you fail or weren't the best at some point in time, it certainly wasn't all a waste of time. The growth mindset allows jiu-jitsu practitioners to value what they are doing along the way. They value the setbacks, the challenges, the learning, and the growth. They are constantly problem solving and trying to make forward progress through the feedback of the day. Maybe you aren't a blackbelt yet in jiu-jitsu, in business, or in life right now, but the learning along the way should be deeply meaningful and satisfying.

Principle 2: Momentum

"Success is like a snowball... It takes momentum to build and the more you roll in the right direction, the bigger it gets." – Steve Ferrante

Nobody has a perfectly smooth and easy path to success in life. In fact, some have a lot more obstacles to overcome than others.   Imagine being born in a country such as Czechoslovakia, a country formed in 1918 and laid to rest in 1993 when it was divided into two separate nations, the Czech Republic and Slovakia. The former Czechoslovakia was a country that was no stranger to political turmoil and unrest. Pulled between Nazi Germany and the communist Soviet Union, it was a struggling landlocked nation familiar with war and uncertainty that always fought for democracy, sometimes winning, but often losing. Few people can claim to be from a country that in the current global world order simply does not exist anymore.

We all have struggles in life. We have struggles with health, relationships, finances, wondering about things like fulfillment, and what we want to be when we grow up. To this day in many parts of the world, there are millions of people who struggle with the core essentials of life itself; food, water, security, or anything that would appear on the bottom of the most basic human needs for survival. That's everyday life in war torn geographies where you have no idea what tomorrow will bring. That sort of uncertainty can become overwhelmingly stressful and debilitating.

But this is the exact situation that the Pravec family found itself in which included their young son Karel. Karel's father was a government employee with a good job and responsibilities. In a country constantly in a state of flux with political leadership changing hands regularly and power struggles that ensued, people who were once on the inside with good jobs could quickly find themselves on the outside of the good graces of any new government leaders. This ultimately was the case with Karel's father who found himself out of a job when a new government was formed. Fortunately, Karel's father was resourceful, determined, and clever. The family would escape the communist country in 1980, make their way through the former Yugoslavia and into Austria before landing safely in the United States later that year in 1980.

Karel Pravec flocked to the disciplines of the martial arts upon arrival in the United States beginning Tae Kwon Do, which was an art that was readily available in the greater New York and New Jersey area where the family settled. He would train striking seven days a week while working and attending school eventually earning an MBA from Columbia University. He was now an immigrant Ivy League educated man working a professional job in corporate finance. But he was like metal to a magnet with his martial arts pursuits.

Decades ago, information was a precious commodity. There was no internet, eBooks, or mobile phones. Pravec stumbled upon a VHS tape of Gracie Jiu-Jitsu in 1991 which led him to attend a weekend seminar in New Jersey organized by the legendary members of the Gracie family, Rorion, Rickson, Helio, and Royce. A few short years later, it would be Renzo Gracie that started navigating to the greater New York and New Jersey area for one month stretches at schools that were being opened by Craig Kukuk. Renzo began doing private lessons and seminars at Kukuk's schools heading back and forth between Brazil and the New Jersey area.

Kukuk to this day is a lesser known but instrumental figure in jiu-jitsu history. Kukuk was the very first U.S. native to achieve the rank of black belt in Brazilian Jiu-Jitsu in 1992. Kukuk was raised in California, was a high-school wrestler, and joined the infamous Gracie Academy in Torrance, California in the 1980's training under Rorion Gracie up to brown belt. It was Rorion that talked Kukuk into traveling to Brazil to gain immersive jiu-jitsu experience at the Gracie Academy in Rio de Janeiro, ultimately earning his black belt under Royler Gracie.

It was Kukuk who made his way east opening schools on the east coast and partnering with Renzo Gracie. The two would go on to produce and publish the very first jiu-jitsu instructional sold to the American audience. But after a falling out, it would be Renzo that went on to achieve jiu-jitsu infamy with both his personal fighting career and long-standing academy, while Kukuk was relegated to obscurity in the jiu-jitsu history books. If you were to ask most jiu-jitsu practitioners who Craig Kukuk is, they would look at you with complete cluelessness.

Pravec began his official jiu-jitsu training under Kukuk and through Kukuk he was introduced to the charismatic and lovable Renzo Gracie. Renzo would go on to establish the famed Renzo Gracie Academy in Manhattan, and it was Pravec that would become one of his very first students joining even before other notables at the Academy such as John Danaher and Matt Serra.

Pravec, by his own admission, was a slow learner. He tended to overthink things and had what he described as "very long and painful" slumps in his progression. But he never gave up and built up momentum over time. It was a hard environment. You were forced to sink or swim back then. Everybody was constantly thrown into the fire. Pravec, a scrawny white-collar corporate worker already well into his 30's was rolling with the younger, larger, and more athletic students including Shawn Williams, Matt Serra, John Danaher, and Master Renzo Gracie.

Pravec's success in jiu-jitsu is clearly along the adage, "slow and steady wins the race." It was the momentum that he started early in his career that allowed him to build upon and grow as a practitioner.

Pravec's story is an amazing one and worthy of admiration from anyone who feels that they are starting late in life, or with obstacles and barriers to overcome. Ryan Ford, the host of the hugely popular Grappling Central Podcast, featured the legendary practitioner now known as "SilverFox" on a podcast episode. The podcast allowed others to listen in like a fly on the wall and gain insight into the importance of building momentum on the mats, in business, and in life. To hear Pravec share and document his story with Ford is a gift and a treasure to those seeking clues to the principles required for success in life.

Pravec would transition out of corporate finance and ultimately dedicate his life to the learning and teaching of jiu-jitsu at his academy in New Jersey and teaching very popular seminars around the globe. "SilverFox" is a good description for Pravec. He has a small frame, short brush cut haircut, and a face that says, "I've seen a lot in life." Life has provided him with wisdom that most will never acquire due to his personal life experiences. He's certainly a father-figure to those he touches, and the mid-50's practitioner looks to be ready to continue his role as the ultimate global ambassador of the art that has changed his life.

Jiu-Jitsu Is One Big Globally Related Family

Since jiu-jitsu is still such a young sport, and one with clear lineage back to Brazil, it doesn't take much effort to connect practitioners using the six degrees of separation. The six degrees of separation is the idea that all living people in the world are six or fewer steps away from each other so that a chain of "a friend of a friend" statements can be made to connect any two people in a maximum of six steps.

The six degrees of separation was originally proposed by Frigyes Karinthy in 1929 but popularized in a 1990 play written by John Guare. In jiu-jitsu, it rarely takes more than two or three degrees of separation to connect any two practitioners. For example, we can take two practitioners in this chapter and play the six degrees game to demonstrate how connected we really are to one another as an extended global jiu-jitsu family. Ryan Ford, the host of the industry leading Grappling Central Podcast, is a jiu-jitsu practitioner in Atlanta, Georgia and was interviewing Karel Pravec, the practitioner from New Jersey. Pravec studied directly under Renzo Gracie. Renzo had another student who trained and eventually became a UFC fighter and a black belt that would eventually move to Atlanta, Georgia to set up his own academy in Suwanee, GA. Ryan Ford would become a student at this Renzo Gracie affiliate academy thus connecting Ford to Pravec in only two degrees of separation between the common denominator of Renzo Gracie. Practitioners around the world should realize that we are all one big jiu-jitsu family with very few degrees of separation from one another.

Jiu-Jitsu Pilgrimages

Pravec, training at the epicenter of east coast jiu-jitsu at the Renzo Academy, would have a front row seat to the countless high-level athletes that make their way to Manhattan to improve their jiu-jitsu. It's important to understand some of the unwritten and unofficial rituals that are symbolic of one's journey in jiu-jitsu for the serious practitioner. "Hajj" is an Arabic term to describe an annual pilgrimage to Mecca, the holiest city for Muslims and a mandatory religious duty for Muslims that must be carried out at least once in their lifetime by all adult Muslims who can make the journey both financially and physically.

Such is the case with a pilgrimage to the Renzo Gracie Academy in New York at some point in your jiu-jitsu lifetime. This is the place where the very best develop and converge. It is a place of refinement. It is a place of solidarity. It is a place of symbolism, and it is a place of submission.

Whereas Muslims can also go to Mecca to perform rituals at other times of the year (referred to as "lesser pilgrimage"), jiu-jitsu practitioners can make lesser or more frequent pilgrimages to the Renzo Gracie Academy in New York. Top athletes come for days, weeks, or months to supplement their training with the very best in the sport. Some athletes will travel multiple times a year to train at the academy. The logistical problems, expenses, and inconveniences are just sacrifices to be made to improve your momentum as a practitioner.

One such athlete that made countless pilgrimages to the Renzo Gracie Academy becoming a friend and training partner to Pravec was Firas Zahabi, the famed coach of multiple champions including one of the greatest martial arts fighters of all time Georges St. Pierre. Zahabi is one of those rare mythical wizards of fighting and is the head coach at Tristar Gym, itself a petri-dish to developing top martial art talents. It was Zahabi and St. Pierre that would be the ones making as many pilgrimages to Manhattan as often as they could. Zahabi lives in Montreal, Quebec, Canada. If you think you have a long commute to your jiu-jitsu academy, think again. It's doubtful you must pass international borders and go through Customs and U.S. Border Patrol to refine your jiu-jitsu game.

Zahabi is a cerebral practitioner much like John Danaher, a legendary instructor and the very man who awarded Zahabi his jiu-jitsu black belt at the Renzo Gracie Academy. Both are avid students of philosophy. Zahabi's bachelor's degree is in philosophy. Zahabi strongly believes in living life and practicing the arts through principles of success. He takes a very intellectual approach to the arts. Zahabi believes that jiu-jitsu is about problem solving. It requires figuring things out while under pressure. You can learn a million techniques. The possibilities are infinitely endless. But there is no way one can cover every single thing that can happen in a fight.

Jiu-jitsu is about learning how to understand and make decisions on your own. That's where mastering the principles of success come into play. Principles allow you to make those good decisions on your own. In life, when you make a bad decision, you pay for it. When you make a good decision, you profit from it. Jiu-jitsu is no different. You must use your brain. It's all about making good decisions.

Implementing Momentum

Zahabi believes in the principle of momentum to build your mind and body for success. Momentum is the secret ingredient to success. Once you figure out the power of momentum, everything will fall into place, and the results will just take over. Long-term success in anything in life requires momentum. Pro golfers didn't get great overnight. They didn't master a swing in one day. It is only through momentum that they end up mastering the game.

What most people want in life are fast results. They want the quick gains, the short-cuts, the fast-track. What most don't realize though is that it is through principles like momentum that the fastest long-term gains are made. Momentum means that you don't become a flame-out or a quitter. It's about making changes that will last a lifetime.

Momentum is all about starting with something small. Sometimes even super small. You may even start so small that people wonder, "What's the point?" But the point is that the key to long-term success is building momentum and the only way to build momentum over a lifetime is if it becomes a habit.

Success is about creating incremental improvements through the power of momentum. Small changes keep adding up to larger improvements. Larger improvements over time lead to personal transformation. Your jiu-jitsu game will be no different. Start with small changes and keep building training and technique momentum.

Momentum then is like a snowball. It starts out small. But as it starts rolling downhill, it picks up speed and power. It just keeps growing until the energy is unstoppable. You never want to get in the way of something that has momentum whether it is a monster snowball or a fast-moving freight train. But even the freight train had to start out barely moving and note how much energy it takes to get momentum going on a freight train. But then you can't stop it. That's what you are doing for yourself. You will be making yourself unstoppable in life through the power of momentum.

The same applies in business and in life. In his 2008 book "The Momentum Effect: How to Ignite Exceptional Growth," author J.C. Larreche lays out the research on how some companies have discovered the secret to sustained high growth environments. The secret? It's the principle of momentum. Those businesses have learned how to create the conditions that lead to exceptional organic growth which feeds on itself, moving the entity forward with greater force.

Individuals can apply this same proven principle that Zahabi teaches to his champion caliber fighters. It is about creating a winning framework for building momentum, keeping it for a lifetime, and harnessing its immense power.

Momentum leads to higher self-satisfaction and positive engagement in life. Happiness is increased because you know you are moving closer to your goals and objectives with each passing day through the power of momentum allowing you to grow as a person in jiu-jitsu, in business, and in life.

Momentum is about starting with very small action items, and at times they may even appear to be insignificant or too easy. But they are designed to build momentum. Maybe it is working on your foot placement while in guard, or better posture while in the guard of an opponent. Each day, you will improve upon something that seems so easy to do. But day after day, you just keep improving by 1%. Days become weeks, weeks become months, and months become years. 1% improvements compound and start stacking up like mountains, and that is the magic of momentum.

The lessons of momentum taught by Zahabi are life changing. Karel Pravec applied the principle of momentum in his struggles in jiu-jitsu and life as an immigrant to the United States with great success. Ryan Ford applied the principle of momentum in developing a grappling focused podcast from scratch. The principle of momentum can and should be applied to all areas of your life but specifically to your health, jiu-jitsu, and career pursuits. Start small and build momentum.

Principle 3: Consistency

"It's not what we do once in a while that shapes our lives. It's what we do consistently." – Tony Robbins

Just a few short years ago, Vince "Bear" Quitugua had a serious problem. Quitugua had started a clothing company that focused on streetwear and his passion for jiu-jitsu. Quitugua, a jiu-jitsu black belt, loved surfing, skateboarding, and creativity. He was also ambitious. But raw ambition alone doesn't equate to ultimate success.

Quitugua's clothing line wasn't popular, and he was starting to question whether the time and energy was worth it. Even Jake McKee, the Budo Videos CEO who had early distribution rights acknowledged that the clothing line wasn't moving. It just sat in their warehouse collecting dust. Inventory is the curse of a distributor business. Inventory is money. Inventory is space that could be used for other products that sell. And now it was Quitugua who was thinking about his wife and kids and how being an entrepreneur sounds great right up until you find yourself without benefits, insurance, and a steady paycheck to put food on the table.

Quitugua was no stranger to hardship and sacrifice. Born in California but raised in Guam, his childhood was spent in a homemade structure with wooden walls and a leaky tarp for a roof. Puddles would form on the floor on rainy days. The family knew that any home not made of concrete was a candidate for complete destruction from any future typhoon that could hit the island country. Imagine how it would feel to ponder what day your family house would no longer exist because it was wiped off the dirt that it was parked on and blown into obscurity.

Today, the jiu-jitsu world is very familiar with Quitugua's company Shoyoroll. It has a cult like following and sponsors some of the biggest stars in the jiu-jitsu space. The running joke of the successful is that it takes at least ten years to become an overnight success. Now the limited edition gi's sell out within minutes.

Thousands of fans and customers around the world anxiously wait for the next "drop" to happen where they all rush to and often crash the website hoping to get lucky against fellow buyers who want the same piece of upscale jiu-jitsu fashionwear.

Building a million-dollar company requires consistency even in the face of adversity when it often appears to be hopeless. Pat Tenore has loudly proclaimed, "Shoyoroll rules!" If there is another person that understands the struggles that people go through, it's Pat M. Tenore. Tenore is the creator and founder of another breakthrough clothing company, RVCA, which he founded in 2001 out of his garage.

Tenore, much like Quitugua, spent the early part of his life in poverty outside of San Francisco. Raised by a single mother, the family often subsided on food stamps. Tenore was good at surfing, skating, designing clothes and art. Tenore was only nineteen years of age when his son Joseph was born. He didn't go to college, and everything was done through self-education and personal tenacity. He, like many other struggling businessmen, knew about drudgery, hardship, and personal beatdowns.

RVCA would go on to become a $50 million a year company with over 200 "advocates" which are artists, musicians, models, and other talent sponsored individuals who participate in the rising brand.

The universe has a beautiful way of merging creative designs. It would be an epic design collaboration between RVCA founder PM Tenore and Shoyoroll founder Vince "Bear" Quitugua that led to a special edition Mendes Brothers RVCA/Shoyoroll Gi in September of 2016.

The Mendes Brothers, Rafael and Guilherme, are human works of jiu-jitsu art. This description is quite fitting even for their jiu-jitsu academy appropriately called "AOJ," which stands for "The Art of Jiu-Jitsu." Watching the Mendes brothers roll in jiu-jitsu is like watching indoor cigarette smoke make its way around a fixated object with the slightest of air movement. The illusion is that the smoke is there one moment and gone the next. You can see it, but you can't really touch it.

Rafa Mendes is like a ghost made of smoke that can choke you, but you can't fight back because it's like he was never there in the first place. Rolling with Rafa is like the initial moments upon waking from a very bad dream. There's a split second where you can't quite tell if you experienced something that was real, or if it was all just a nightmare and product of your imagination.

Rafael Mendes is a black belt under Ramon Lemos. He is a phenomenal grappler and started to excel in high profile tournaments as a late teenager. When it comes to accomplishments in competitive grappling, Rafa Mendes is in very rare company. He is a two-time IBJJF Pan American Champion, a three-time IBJJF European Champion, a two-time ADCC Champion, and a record setting six-time IBJJF World Champion in the featherweight division. Rafa Mendes was one of the few grapplers that was able to beat the great Rubens "Cobrinha" Charles Maciel in competition.

The Mendes brothers grew up in Rio Claro, a sub-city of Sao Paulo, Brazil. As early teenagers, the parents of the boys split, leaving them without a real father figure. It would be Ramon Lemos, the man who would later become the leader of the now well established and highly regarded Atos Jiu-Jitsu team that would fill that role for the young boys.

What was amazing about the Mendes brothers was their consistent dedication to the art from an early age. They trained multiple times a day, for years. Skills and techniques were layered upon fundamentals. Timing was layered over positions, and human movement was elevated to levels never seen before in the competitive jiu-jitsu world. Rafael Mendes would eventually master movements not normally seen at that time such as creative variations of leg-drags, the Berimbolo, and the 50/50 guard. For his opponents, it was like trying to assemble a puzzle with half the pieces missing while wearing a blindfold. They simply looked out of place, clumsy, and confused by his movements.

Consistency is a very important principle to harness in life. In his highly regarded book, "The Power of Consistency," author Weldon Long shares his insights into how we take actions with the thoughts and beliefs that we consistently have, and the cumulative results of those actions eventually create the quality and circumstances of our lives and businesses. Long has quite the personal story to back up his own insights. He walked out of prison in 2003 only to become broke and homeless. Within 6 years of walking out of jail, he had built an Inc. 5000 company with over $20 million in revenues.

The basic premise of consistency is simple enough and can be applied to jiu-jitsu and other key areas of life. Your success on and off the mats will ultimately come down to how well and how often you do little things that matter. It's not going to be about learning one move, one technique, or one position. It's about doing all the little things correctly and consistently. All those little details, all those little adjustments, and all those little extra efforts will allow the big breakthroughs to happen.

Jiu-Jitsu is a lot like business and life. The growth comes from making mistakes, learning from those mistakes, and then adjusting and refining. The key to faster improvement is in recognizing the error of our ways as quickly and as efficiently as possible and then making those adjustments.

Ralph Waldo Emerson once wrote, "We become what we think about all day long." It becomes critical to think through what it is you want to become in life. What is it you want to achieve on the mats? Do you want to be a fit and healthy practitioner? Are your thoughts leading you to make choices and decisions that will lead you to those outcomes? Or are you concentrating on how you can skip out of work as fast as possible to meet your friends at a bar and eat unhealthy foods?

Principle 3: Consistency   Paul Kindzia

Being consistent is an essential ingredient to your journey in life. Consistency is one of the pillars that will lead you to a life of honor and prosperity. Can you show up to practice consistently? Can you eat healthy foods consistently? Can you concentrate on refining your technique consistently? Can you get to bed on time to recover and obtain adequate sleep consistently? What you do on any given day or within any given week is not the defining characteristic of your destiny. What you do consistently is. That applies to success in all areas of life including personal and business.

The Mendes brothers were talented. They were skilled. They were also fanatically consistent in their training and dedication to their art. They created art on the mats, and it showed when they competed. They had problems along the way. They had limited financial resources. They had a broken home. They had to travel and move to a new country and learn a new language along with new cultures. That didn't stop them from being consistent in the practice of their values and goals.

The Mendes brothers didn't succumb to the challenges of the economy, their competition, or their personal constraints. They did not wait for their obstacles to magically disappear so that they could claim their glory. They did not stay home and become stagnant. They were always pushing themselves, reaching further, and moving forward. Theirs is a story of overcoming challenges and finding a way to succeed and prosper regardless of the roadblocks that were in front of them.

It's best to begin with a mindset of consistency. One of the keys to the Mendes brothers' success was their consistent discipline in creating a winning mindset that allowed them to thrive and grow in the face of adversity. Rafael didn't sit around

40

and wait for the great Cobrinha to retire. He elevated his game to that of Cobrinha rather than waiting for things to magically get better.

What holds back most jiu-jitsu practitioners is not a lack of information on techniques. Between digital courses, YouTube videos, competition footage, and personal instructors at their school, the information is there for everybody to learn from. Improvement, or lack thereof, isn't due to the lack of information, it's really a problem with a lack of action. Most practitioners aren't doing the things they know they should be doing on a consistent basis. It's a consistency issue, not a restriction of information.

Results in life are usually a reflection of your actions. Your actions are the result of your emotions. Your emotions are the result of what your personal beliefs are. More specifically, what it is you believe to be true. If you think you don't have time for exercise and jiu-jitsu, then you won't make the time for exercise and jiu-jitsu. If you believe that you have bad "fat" genetics and that what you eat doesn't matter, you will eat poorly. If you believe that you will feel "good enough" tomorrow if you stay up past midnight each evening rather than going to bed early, then you will lack sleep and rest. Thus, it becomes important, even critical, that your beliefs are strongly rooted in positive behaviors that could lead to consistent actions that will eventually lead to personal success.

Is It An Art Gallery Or A Training Academy?

Under the watchful eye of the sun with a fitting palm tree that stands as if it were the Eiffel Tower in Paris sits a nondescript white building on 17th Street in Costa Mesa, California. Inside the white rectangular structure with glass windows lining the front street side is The Art Of Jiu-Jitsu, an academy founded in July of 2012 as a collaborative effort between the Mendes Brothers and RVCA founder PM Tenore.

The objective of the project was simple, spread the wonders of the jiu-jitsu lifestyle and make a positive impact on the community. What makes this shrine so different than any other academy is multiple factors. First, in quintessential California style, the school sits only about a mile from Newport Beach along the coast, just nestled between Huntington Beach which is to the north and Laguna Beach to the south. The academy does not have punching bags, boxing gloves, or other MMA type training equipment. "AOJ" as it is known, is pure jiu-jitsu. But finally, the biggest differentiator of the Art of Jiu-Jitsu Academy is the fact, as its name implies, is actually a work of art. Walk in, and you will see crisp white walls, pristine mats, and yes, actual black and white artwork on the walls. The only thing missing from this gallery of excellence is an elderly red blazer wearing security guard telling visitors not to touch anything from the other side of a red velvet rope. This mix of jiu-jitsu and heaven makes it seem as if you are training in an art museum. AOJ cannot be any more fitting than it is.

This facility is sacred space, worthy of legacies, visionaries, and originals. It's the home of champions. The universe delivered us carbon, oxygen, DNA, and now the Art of Jiu-Jitsu. Inside these four walls contain two of the greatest competitors to put on a jiu-jitsu gi who are now teaching the next generations of practitioners under their guidance.

It is Rafael Mendes who shares his pearls with the next generation of young practitioners who listen intently to his words. "Champions do more. They have a different mindset. They are willing to sacrifice whatever it takes. That's the difference between a champion and somebody else." AOJ is the holy place to make the techniques crisp and sharp and fix the little mistakes made in sparring which allows students to apply everything when it counts in competition.

Rafael believes that talent can aid in the journey, but it isn't just talent, you must be consistent. You must have vision because it isn't just a dream, it is something that you are doing every single day. As a six-time featherweight world champion, something that has never been done before, Rafael Mendes has already secured his legacy as a competitor, but what is unknown is the impact that he and his brother Gui will have on the sport of jiu-jitsu for years to come.

What Quitugua, Tenore, and the Mendes brothers show us is that consistent actions are required for an abundant and successful life. Where your thoughts go, so do your actions. Where your actions go, so do your results. Taking responsibility for your actions is the catalyst between being consistent and being inconsistent. Being consistent will not always feel comfortable. It will at times feel mundane, uneventful, even non-exciting. But it is the consistency in your life that will make or break your future results.

The key is consistent action. It is not any single grand motion or effort that will allow you to reach your dreams. It is doing a lot of little things regularly that are going to make the biggest difference. Your life and career will not be defined nor determined by the moments of recognition that everybody else sees. Your life will be defined by the little moments of action that nobody else sees. Your life will be defined by your consistency.

Principle 4: Discipline

"You will never have a greater or lessor dominion than that over yourself... the height of a man's success is gauged by his self-mastery; the depth of his failure by his self-abandonment. ...And this law is the expression of eternal justice. He who cannot claim dominion over himself will have no dominion over others." – Leonardo da Vinci

Jean Jacques Machado has described jiu-jitsu as more than just a martial art. For those who are fortunate enough to have exposure to the practice, jiu-jitsu is a way to learn how to overcome life's challenges. Machado describes jiu-jitsu in those terms. It is a way of living and looking at life itself.

It's this all-in mentality and spiritual approach to jiu-jitsu that has made Machado one of the finest grappling instructors in the world. Machado is a coral belt in jiu-jitsu which is the highest grandmaster level of the practice. A coral belt in jiu-jitsu can only be given once a Brazilian Jiu-Jitsu black belt reaches the seventh degree. That is a multi-decade achievement beyond achieving the status of a normal black belt. In karate or Tae

45

Kwon Do, there may be thousands upon thousands of black belts around the world claiming to be "masters of the art." There are less than fifty coral belts in jiu-jitsu around the entire globe. Jean Jacques Machado and two of his brothers are each one of those rare few.

Teaching the lessons of life through jiu-jitsu is the goal that Machado has mastered as he looks to positively impact the lives of his students on and off the mats. It's his wisdom, knowledge, and experience that can be passed on to others to help them make changes in their own lives both on and off the mats.

Machado is no stranger to adversity. A nephew of Gracie jiu-jitsu co-founder and master Carlos Gracie, Sr., Jean Jacques was one of five Machado brothers that learned the art from a very early age. There was one significant difference between Jean Jacques and his brothers though. Jean Jacques Machado suffered from birth defects because of Amniotic Band Syndrome, a condition that left him with only the thumb and the little finger on his left hand.

Despite the congenital condition and the inability to fully grip with the left hand, normally a required element of submission grappling, Machado improvised his game to turn the weakness into a strength. Machado became very effective at taking the back of opponents, which in jiu-jitsu terms is a series of maneuvers and techniques that allow one competitor to get behind their opponent. Being on the back of an opponent allows for more direct access to the neck for choking from behind. It creates vulnerability. Opponents found it quite difficult to stop Machado from slipping in the rear naked choke using his left hand once he had established position on the back side of them.

The deformed left hand became a weapon. It was like a wood splitting wedge that separated the chin from the chest of a defensive opponent and exposed the throat to chokes from behind.

When Reputations Are Made

On May 29th, 2005 Machado would come out of a four-year retirement from competition to participate in a super fight at the Long Beach California Abu Dhabi. Abu Dhabi Combat Club (ADCC) events are grappling competitions involving professional athletes at the highest level of submission grappling. They are the equivalent to having a world series type tournament that could be described as the greatest submission and grappling tournaments ever created. It is the Super Bowl of submission grappling. The participants, a mix of invitees and winners of qualifying events, are those at the highest levels of luta livre, wrestling, judo, jiu-jitsu, sambo, shooto, and other grappling based mixed martial arts.

Machado would headline the event against a young up and comer from San Diego, California that was building quite a reputation for himself by the name of Dean Lister. Lister at the time had been called the "World's Greatest Grappler" based on his performance at the Abu Dhabi in 2003 in which he submitted three of his four opponents going on to win the absolute title in remarkable fashion.

Lister was the son of a US Marine and grew up like a lot of military kids, bouncing around from one location to another. He spent time in Central and South America finding social sanctuary in grappling, eventually becoming a standout wrestler in high school and a Sambo champion before officially getting into Brazilian jiu-jitsu in 1995.

What made Lister a spectacle was his relentless pursuit of submissions at every moment during matches. Where many competitors relied on a more conservative strategy of playing for points and the favors of the referee's by controlling positions, Lister never had any desire to leave things in the hands of judges or scorecards. He hunted for game killing submissions, but some of his favorite submissions were referred to as leg locks, something that wasn't particularly popular or prevalent in those days of submission grappling.

Leg locks continue to be a paradoxical and controversial anomaly within the sport of jiu-jitsu. Early practitioners of Brazilian jiu-jitsu that were brought up through the Gracie lineage of the sport derided the techniques as lowly suburban techniques. Early Gracie's catered their academies to the upper classes in Rio de Janeiro and Sao Paulo and frowned upon these techniques while training in kimonos, referred to as Gi's in the jiu-jitsu world.

Other early instructors of jiu-jitsu favored leg attacks. One example of this was Oswaldo Fadda in the 1950's. Fadda was one of the only individuals that earned a red belt from a non-Gracie lineage and didn't charge tuition for his jiu-jitsu classes at the time. Fadda held practices in public places catering to Brazil's poor. Kimonos (Gi's) were expensive to purchase and keep clean. Fadda focused on what could now be described as "no-Gi" jiu-jitsu and was an advocate of using leglocks as an effective submission technique.

Fast forward a few decades, and many jiu-jitsu practitioners continued to neglect and frown upon leg locks as the kind of dangerous, dirty, and cheap techniques that only the under-privileged would use, which still influences tournament rules to this day. But Lister wasn't influenced by the perception of foot locks and leg attacks by many of his Gracie lineage competitors at the time. Lister embraced any and all techniques that would force a man to quit or possibly become disabled. It was a choice that competitors against Lister would have to make in the heat of battle. Either tap out to the submission or risk permanent damage to joints, ligaments, tendons, and bones. Neck-cranks, heel hooks, and wrist locks were all fair game in Lister's world, and the man started acquiring the nickname "The Boogeyman" as opponents began to mysteriously get injured and drop out of future scheduled fights with Lister rather than face him in competition and risk what could end up being a career ending injury.

On that fateful day of May 29th in 2005, Lister built upon his ever-growing legacy as he beat Machado by points and was able to perform basic techniques at a very high level. Lister would go on to become a very formidable grappling and MMA opponent winning multiple ADCC championships, two U.S. National Sambo championships, a mixed martial arts King of the Cage Middleweight championship, along with being a six-time competitor in the UFC racking up an impressive 4-2 UFC fight record.

For all that Lister has accomplished in competition, Lister is less known for his teaching accomplishments. Lister would go on to coach, teach, and rank several high-profile martial artists and submission specialists. But one would stand out as being more unique than others.

A Master Promotes His Student

Lister awarded a black belt to a passionate student by the name of John Gretton Willink. Willink can be described physically as a giant steel fire hydrant, with a concrete base, a permanent scowl, but a funny and inspiring demeanor. He's a 5'11" 235-pound muscular powerhouse. A testosterone laden man's man with piercing eyes. If the heavens created a template for the modern-day version of a Hollywood movie special forces commando, the mold would have been made with Willink's likeness.

Willink was given the nickname "Jocko" by his parents even before his birth. To this day, "Jocko" is growing into a brand all to his own. You know you are a sensation when you can join the short list of historical mononymous persons whereby millions of people instantly know who you are by reference to one name only. Examples would include Madonna, Plato, Oprah, Sting, Michelangelo, Bono and now Jocko.

Jocko is known for many things. He's a top podcaster with his wildly popular long form Jocko Podcast. He is a retired United States Navy Seal and was commander of SEAL Team Three's Task Unit Bruiser during the Battle of Ramadi in Iraq. He is a New York Times bestselling author, a founder of the management consulting firm Echelon Front, and entrepreneur that has sales of products ranging from T-shirts to a multi-million-dollar enterprise that sells White Pomegranate Tea called Jocko White Tea (for Jocko fans, it's GOOD). Jocko is also a co-owner of Victory MMA, a massive 22,000 square foot state of the art training facility that offers over 130 classes each week to area residents together with Dean Lister.

Jocko began training jiu-jitsu in 1995 under Fabio Santos. Santos, a multi-time World Champion and Pan American Champion in his own right was a Rickson Gracie blackbelt that began teaching at the infamous Rorion Gracie academy in Torrance California upon immigrating to the United States. Santos eventually moved to San Diego, California, a city that was across the bay from the Naval Amphibious Base Coronado, the renowned base and training facility for United States Navy SEALs. Blessed by geographical proximity, the rest is history as Jocko was hooked on the adrenaline rush of making grown men physically submit right from the start of his introduction to the art.

To succeed in jiu-jitsu, one needs a tremendous amount of discipline, which wasn't in short supply for Jocko. Being a special forces commando relies on discipline. Without it, there wouldn't be anyway applicants could progress through Basic Underwater Demolition/SEAL training (BUD/S), which has over an 80 percent attrition rate. Jocko thrived in the environment and when asked about the difficulties of progressing through BUD/S training stated, "It's a lot of running and pushups and eating a lot of food and watching other people quit. Those are some of my favorite things."

The Importance Of Discipline

The term, "discipline" has been used for thousands of years from many philosophers, historical leaders, and warriors alike. There is a full list of quotes about discipline that has stood the test of time and would include those from the likes of Ralph Waldo Emerson, George Washington, Dalai Lama XIV, Theodore Roosevelt, Harry Truman, Buddha, Plato, Horace, and Aristotle. In quick fashion, Jocko seems to have figured out a way to make the word discipline not only his personal mantra but the foundation of his personal brand. A man may not be able to physically "own" a word in the English language, but Jocko seems to have figured out how to take possession of the stadium rights to it. Jocko is human discipline as if the word was tattooed across his forehead for all to see it.

Jocko is the epitome of the type of man that other men dream about being. He's a pseudo-father-figure to the lost souls who need assistance following a clearer life compass. Through his books, podcasts, videos, and social media posts, it is the message and lessons about the benefits of personal discipline that blare out as if he has a personal megaphone up to the ears of those that follow him.

Self-discipline is the ability of a person to self-guide and shape their behaviors to remain focused on personal goals and objectives. Discipline should be implemented into your daily practice in life. Being disciplined applies to those areas that are the foundations of success which include, but are not limited to, sleep habits, training habits, eating habits, time management, and work.

Discipline adds value to your life by offering those that exercise it with more freedom. Ask yourself these questions;

- Are you likely to have more or less money if you are financially disciplined?
- Are you likely to have more or less free time if you are disciplined with your time?
- Are you likely to have better or worse health if you are physically disciplined?
- Are you likely to have more or less professional success if you are disciplined with your career work?

If you want better results in your jiu-jitsu, get more disciplined with all the factors that would assist you in your goals; your sleep, your diet, your finances, your time management, your commitment to practice.

Success in life is often believed to be based on intrinsic gifts and natural talents. But advanced jiu-jitsu practitioners know that is not the case. Success is based on the willingness to do what needs to be done, day after day, consistently with focus and intent. Transforming your jiu-jitsu abilities don't happen by themselves, even by watching hundreds of hours of YouTube technique videos from your couch. The breakthroughs happen on the mats, in the trenches, with willing partners who are sharing the blood, sweat, and tears required for progress to be made. There is no substitution for mat time and that mat time is contingent upon the personal discipline to show up ready to roll each practice and exert yourself mentally and physically.

The path to success is a long one. Jiu-jitsu belts are earned over extended periods of time. Those belts aren't handed out in vending machines or purchased from a mall cart salesman. They are earned over the years from the discipline to set yourself on the path of success and stay on that path of success. The path to jiu-jitsu success is a hard path. It's a relentless path. It's a path that requires persistent discipline to not veer off when the times get tough, and the distractions become many.

Discipline has two components to it; the mental and the physical. It takes mental discipline to ensure that your actions get executed. Thinking alone won't get you to the promised land. Nor will it change or transform your life. It's only through taking physical action after having the mental discipline to stay focused where the magic adds up day after day.

Jiu-jitsu can change your life. It has transformed the lives of thousands of men and women who have walked the path of discipline through the art. Through discipline, you learn to navigate the challenges of life that include stress, regret, disappointment, failure, losing, and breakdown. But it's through discipline that you learn the root of all good qualities. It's learning to control yourself and overcome the feelings and emotions of the moment. Your feelings and emotions will play games with you. They will trick you into making bad decisions. Feelings and emotions can trick you into regret. Feelings and emotions can take your ego hostage. Discipline reigns those influences in and stabilizes your intents.

For Jocko, it's clear that discipline has become his best friend. He has built his life around it. It takes care of him like nothing else in the world. It keeps him on the path of strength, health, intelligence, and happiness.

Jiu-jitsu is the outlet that allows you to exercise yourself both physically and mentally. You become strong and flexible through jiu-jitsu. Jiu-jitsu helps you develop your explosive energy and your endurance. It is an excellent physical conditioning program unto itself.

For Jocko, training jiu-jitsu is an incredible thing. Jiu-jitsu is the teaching mechanism that allows one to develop their discipline because it takes discipline to get on the mats day after day, week after week, month after month, and year after year. You may be interested in jiu-jitsu. You may even have a passion for the art and be committed, but there is no way that you will feel like practicing each and every day. You must find the discipline even when you don't feel like it, and you must do it. You must show up at classes, bite down on the mouth guard, and roll with your partners.

It's one thing to preach and write about discipline, it's another to live it – authentically. Nobody questions the authenticity of the gravelly voiced Jocko. Each morning, his Instagram photo is straightforward; a picture of the Timex Ironman wristwatch that displays the time he arose from bed. It varies a few minutes each day but normally clocks in around 4:30am Pacific Time. That's seven days a week and 365 days a year. The caption for the photo is also something short and sweet such as, "Get after it," or "Attack." That's not the behavior of someone faking discipline.

The lessons of discipline through the lens of Jocko is clear; you can be married, you can have four kids, you can be financially stable, you can be healthy, you can write books, you can record weekly podcasts, you can own successful businesses, you can get adequate sleep, and you can train jiu-jitsu if you have the discipline to control yourself. If you want to maximize your jiu-jitsu journey, business, and life, learn to conduct yourself with maximum discipline on and off the mats. Be disciplined with your sleep, your work, your diet, your time management, your finances, and your commitment to your goals and objectives. As Jocko says, "Discipline is freedom."

Principle 5: Principles

"The value of a principle is the number of things it will explain." – Ralph Waldo Emerson

Ray Dalio is a name that very few jiu-jitsu practitioners are familiar with. Did he win IBJJF Pans? No. Did he win ADCC in some years past? No. Is he a black belt direct from Helio Gracie lineage? No.

Dalio founded an investment firm called Bridgewater Associates in 1975 out of his two-bedroom apartment in New York City. Fast forward over forty years, and Bridgewater is one of the top five most important privately held companies in the United States. Bridgewater is a hedge fund. A giant hedge fund, managing over $115 billion in assets under management serving institutional clients including hedge funds, endowments, foundations, foreign governments, and central banks. The hedge fund is the world's largest with over 1,700 employees and has made more money for investors than any other hedge fund in history.

What set Dalio apart from other people in business and in life was his fascination and application of personal principles. Dalio is to this day obsessed with principles. He strongly believes that principles are the reasons behind his financial success and sees principles as the success factor in people pursuing various meaningful endeavors.   Dalio, now approaching 70 years of age and worth over $17 billion dollars, is the author of a book on his life's work, appropriately titled, "Principles: Life and Work."

Principles, as Dalio explains in his book, are fundamental truths that serve as the foundation for behaviors that get you what you want out of life. Principles can repeatedly be applied in life to help you achieve your goals.

Each of us is faced with thousands of decisions and situations that we must address. Without principles serving as a guide, it would be as if we are experiencing any situation as a brand new never seen before decision that would create total personal chaos. Having well defined principles ahead of time allows a person to deal with situations efficiently, hopefully allowing them to make the right decisions that lead them one step closer to achieving their goals and objectives.

"Having a good set of principles is like having a good collection of recipes," says Dalio. All successful people operate by principles that help them be successful, though what they choose to be successful at varies enormously, so their principles will vary based on what they will hope to accomplish in life.

To be principled means to consistently operate with principles that can be clearly explained or understood. For most people, that isn't how they operate. They don't have any clearly defined principles that they have thought through. Nor are any principles clearly defined to help them navigate the world around them. Hence, such an unprincipled approach to life does lead to more personal chaos and a lack of accomplishment.

Principles can be developed and applied to any area of life that a person desires. In the field of wealth building, a person may have principles such as; make a substantial living, live below your means by controlling spending, save consistently, eliminate debts, maintain adequate emergency funds, invest prudently over a lifetime, and use proper risk management in all areas of life. These are proven principles of success when it comes to wealth building. Those that choose a life of wealth accumulation will live their lives based upon these principles which have stood the test of time regarding personal finance.

In personal health, a person may have a set of principles to live and make decisions by such as; eat healthy, exercise the body, exercise the mind, gain exposure to sunshine and fresh air, get adequate sleep and rest, reduce stress and anxiety, and avoid harmful substances such as toxins, chemicals, drugs, alcohol, and preservatives in foods. These are proven principles of success when it comes to living a life of health and wellness.

Principles allow for a reasoned person to make decisions quickly and effectively based upon their goals and objectives in life. A person seeking wealth would not live beyond their means and incur reckless debt levels. It would contradict with their pre-determined principles.

Using Principles In Jiu-Jitsu and In Life

Jiu-jitsu can also be approached with a principles-based approach. Examples would include having a survival mindset, always use efficiency of energy, and use natural body movements. These are ones that are taught by Rener Gracie of the famed Gracie Academy in Torrance, California. Rener Gracie and his brother Ryron are very influential members of the jiu-jitsu community albeit with a hint of controversy that gets debated on what the focus of jiu-jitsu should be. Should jiu-jitsu stick to its heritage and legacy as the ultimate self-defense martial art or should the focus yield to the ever growing and popular sport application for competing purposes?

Rener's lineage is as pure as it could get. He is the second eldest son of Grandmaster Rorion Gracie. Rorion is the son of Grandmaster Helio Gracie making Rener the grandson of Helio himself. Rener is a gifted, charismatic, and passionate speaker. He's a tall, charming practitioner with an athletic build that is enviable but far from intimidating. He is a teacher, a mentor, a student, and a philosopher. A lofty handsome man without any signs of the material sprinkles that one would come to expect from a success story. In his wildly popular videos that he shares with the world, there is no fancy Los Angeles haircut, designer clothing, or outlandish jewelry. Rener is most often seen in a jiu-jitsu gi at work or on videos with a short military brush cut haircut and a confident all-natural demeanor.

Rener's concern for jiu-jitsu is that the art is losing its way. He struggles with this at his own academy and at seminars worldwide. Being in his position and upbringing allows him to see how the sport at times is totally watered down. It has veered off course from its fundamental roots. What is changing within the jiu-jitsu world is that sport jiu-jitsu is becoming the emphasis for a lot of people which creates practitioners who have no consideration on how the art would or would not be effective in a real self-defense situation.

It's highly possible in the world of sport jiu-jitsu that a practitioner could earn an advanced color belt and go out in a fight and get beat up badly. The distance that needs to be managed from an opponent in a sport jiu-jitsu match is far different than the distance that needs to be managed in a self-defense situation. In a sporting competition, you can pull a fancy guard or sit in with butterfly hooks while grabbing some sleeves. In a real street fight, you could get knocked out very quickly with that approach.

The odd thing to Rener is that jiu-jitsu took off in popularity when they first saw its effectiveness in the original UFC matches with Royce Gracie, a cousin of Rener. Royce kept his arms out protecting from punches and measuring for distance management during his fights. The world was in awe watching this smaller man defeat much larger opponents in a no-holds barred fighting promotion. Spectators repeatedly saw Royce beating the giant. It was a fantasy dream come true for any person that was bullied on a school bus. Now there was hope in an art that wasn't just mystical fiction.

Nobody walks into the door of the Gracie Academy asking if they could learn how to gain an advantage point over a competitor in a sporting match. They are coming to learn a martial art that could be used effectively against a larger and stronger opponent. Rener's passion is to keep the street self-defense component of jiu-jitsu alive and thriving. He is 100% dedicated to the preservation and perpetuation of the jiu-jitsu that can be used to beat bigger guys in real fights using proven principles of combat. It's the principles that must be mastered.

Like so many masters in jiu-jitsu, Rener is a fan of principles that could be used in various areas of life including sport, health, or business. He is quite the businessman and entrepreneur. Jiu-Jitsu has taught him how to navigate life through principles. One such principle that he employs is excelling in times of comfort and chaos. At one point in his career, Rener severely injured his lower back preventing him from training for over 10 months. It was a serious setback and challenge for a guy that makes his living doing a physical art. He had to overcome that threat to his livelihood. He went into problem solving mode and ultimately created Gracie University Online.

Gracie University was born from the realization that in life, there will be challenges, setbacks, and threats but those problems have already been solved by someone else out there. The techniques to your problems are already out there in this world. You just need to know that they exist. You come to understand that what often appears to be an impossible situation can usually be overcome by a very simple and elegant solution that has already been formulated and tested by somebody else. All problems and challenges are just techniques waiting for you to personally discover.

Gracie University would go on to teach the self-defense aspects of jiu-jitsu to students around the world. All they would need is internet access. This was controversial yet a major innovation at the time in jiu-jitsu. Today, the online program has over 120,000 students in almost 200 countries. It was born out of a personal depression in Rener's life. Have you ever felt like you were struggling with problems that were unsurmountable with no hope in sight? Have you ever felt that the rest of the world did not see things your way causing additional internal and external conflicts in your life?

Acting on principles allowed Rener to turn what often must have felt like a career ending injury into a springboard of enormous opportunity. It was highly unlikely that his life would have played out the way it did were it not for his major back injury and his commitment to personal principles.

An Uncle Like No Other

No one is more pleased with returning the focus of jiu-jitsu back to its roots than Rener's uncle, Rickson Gracie. Students of jiu-jitsu history and the Gracie lineage know that there are a lot of male Gracie family members with names beginning with the letter "R." There are the nine sons of jiu-jitsu Grandmaster Helio Gracie; Rorion, Relson, Rickson, Rolker, Rolyer, Royce, Rerika, Robin, and Ricci. The "R's" are pronounced like "H's" in Portuguese, the native language in Brazil, so Rickson is pronounced, "Hickson." Renzo is pronounced "Henzo." Rener is pronounced "Hener."

Rickson is the third oldest son of Helio but was special in his own way. Rickson was a jiu-jitsu fighter focusing on no-holds barred fights rather than competitive sport jiu-jitsu. He was not a very large man and often competed at 82 kilograms (181 pounds). But he was a strong, overwhelming, and unbreakable human being in a real fight.

The only thing that is debatable is Rickson's final record in all competitions. The common published record for Rickson during his career was 400-0. He was unbeaten in jiu-jitsu competitions, unbeaten in no-holds-barred fights, unbeaten in closed doors fights, and unbeaten in regulated mixed martial arts fights. The only loss that may dispute that unblemished record was a loss in a sport sambo match against Ron Tripp who beat Rickson by points resulting from a throw.

Rickson is like Rener and believes that sport jiu-jitsu is ruining the art of self-defense jiu-jitsu. It is watering down and diluting the art and is leading jiu-jitsu to lose its identity. He fears that jiu-jitsu has now entered a phase at most schools where they completely ignore the art of actual self-defense.

Rickson grew up in a world where training was designed around preparing for the chaos of an actual street fight. Gracie jiu-jitsu was always being challenged as an effective or superior art back during the early days in Brazil. Real fighting was part of the "proof of concept." When the fights broke out, nobody was focused on scoring an advantage point from a well-dressed referee wearing black dress socks while giving hand signals to a scorers table.

There was honor in defending the effectiveness of your martial art during those early decades. In 1994, Rickson competed in Japan to promote the family's legacy outside of Brazil and entered an eight-man tournament called Vale Tudo Japan. It was there that Rickson defeated all his opponents in one night. The wins did more than keep Rickson's record unblemished. They infuriated, tarnished, and dishonored the more famous and reveled Japanese fighters who prided themselves on centuries worth of martial arts combat experience and lineage.

One of those outraged Japanese fighters was Yoji Anjo. Anjo concocted what seemed to be a brilliant plan whereby he would travel all the way to California to regain the pride of the Japanese people by challenging Rickson to a promoted fight back in Japan. Yoji Anjo literally knocked on the front door of the Rickson Gracie Academy unannounced to challenge Rickson who was at home at the time the uninvited guest arrived.

Imagine being at home minding your business with your family and the home phone rings. The person on the other line is someone from your academy explaining that a man came to the academy unannounced, from Japan, and wants to pick a fight...as in right now.

Can you imagine experiencing something like that in your own life? How would it feel to put your shoes on and walk out the door to go meet the physical mystery that awaits you at your place of work? Did Rickson kiss his wife and say goodbye to the kids while saying the typical, "Ok honey, time to go to work. I'll be back later in time for dinner. Have a great day?" And what did Rickson's wife say when this family business madness would erupt? "Ok, I love you too sugar lips. Don't forget that your son Kron has his school play this afternoon?"

But we aren't talking about normal people with normal jobs like bookkeepers and plumbers. This is Rickson Gracie who was in the business of combat, and somebody from the other side of planet Earth had this impulse to prove something. Rickson did what you would imagine any legitimate bad-ass would do. He showed up at the academy and accepted the challenge but with an unexpected twist for Anjo. He was not interested in fighting Anjo in a future promoted fight in Japan with cameras and media. He wanted to fight Anjo on the spot, behind closed doors, and with no media.

Yoji Anjo was now put in an unexpected predicament. He couldn't un-accept his own dramatic challenge made to Rickson. After all, he traveled halfway around the earth to pick a fight. Backing down now under any circumstances would be an awkward and cowardly gesture for any self-proclaimed warrior with any sense of personal pride. It was at this time that Rickson made one of his most famous quotes, "If we fight for money, I'll stop hitting you when you ask me to. If we fight for honor, I'll stop hitting you when I feel like it."

There was only one picture released after the fight to the general public. It was a picture of a bloody faced Anjo being physically assisted by one of his travel companions. The fight was reported as a one-sided beat-down where Rickson passed on the chance to submit Anjo quickly and easily at the beginning of the fight. Rather than ending it quickly, Rickson chose to make a statement to the Japanese at the physical expense of Anjo. The statement was loud, clear, and unambiguous, "This is Gracie jiu-jitsu, and it is superior to anything that the rest of the world has to offer. You may not like it, but you must accept this reality because we have the physical skills to prove it when we feel like it."

Rickson probably went home and had dinner like any other evening with his wife and kids, chewing down a steak while his wife asked, "How was your day today honey?"

Like his nephew Rener, Rickson developed and lived by his own proven principles of success both on and off the mats. Rickson was known for his unique approaches to breathing rooted from his passion for yoga. His work ethic and discipline were unrivaled at the time. Rickson had a singular focus on all things that created the perfect human fighter. He was a man of principle built upon principles. He discovered his own universal truths and expressed those fundamental truths through his principles of fighting. They were his foundations to his behaviors that allowed him to get what he wanted out of life which was simply to be the very best fighter that existed on earth.

He was the rare man that backed up his principles with a repeated willingness to display his proof of concepts. Gracie principles intertwined jiu-jitsu with life in harmony. They believed in using the least amount of force to the greatest effect. That's what productivity is at its core. Be healthy, never quit, exercise daily, don't skip workouts that are good for you, love what you do, sleep to recover, enjoy family, be a good host, and finally win with grace and lose with class. Respect your opponent and learn from your mistakes.

Principle 6: Processes

"If you can't describe what you are doing as a process, you don't know what you're doing." – W. Edwards Deming

Most practitioners wouldn't consider Paducah, Kentucky as any type of hotbed for jiu-jitsu. It's a long way from Brazil, a long way from California, and a long way from just about anywhere one would expect to find any type of significant jiu-jitsu influence on the world. Nestled up against the Ohio River just south of the Illinois border, Paducah is only about 6 miles east of the giant metropolis of Bandana, Kentucky, which itself has a population of 203 lucky residents. It might be fair to state that it's unlikely that the Paducah community will be competing for any major professional sports franchises in the next two million years.

Paducah is a small town of 25,000 residents and was laid out by William Clark of the famed Lewis and Clark Expedition in 1827. Local folklore has it that Clark named the town for the Comanche people, known at the time as the Padoucas. It's a quiet town and an old town. But it is the town that is the home of Three Rivers Martial Arts, a rather unlikely place to produce six of the first forty-eight Royce Gracie Jiu-Jitsu black belts worldwide.

Laying on the mats inside the walls of Three Rivers Martial Arts is Eli Knight, the senior supervising instructor at Three Rivers. He's thinking through and rehearsing technique details that will eventually be recorded on video and uploaded to YouTube. Knight studied Philosophy and English at Murray State University. He's a Royce Gracie jiu-jitsu black belt, and he's trained with some legends including Helio Gracie, Royce Gracie, and Rorion Gracie as well as other top practitioners around the world as part of the Royce Gracie Jiu-Jitsu Network and the G.R.A.C.I.E. law enforcement tactics program.

Producing consistent and value-added videos and sharing them around the world sounds easy but can be tedious and time-consuming. It's one thing to self-record some personal rant on your mobile phone and upload it into the digital never-never-land to receive five accidental views. It's another to pre-plan, record, edit, and upload high quality valued content on a more massive scale. It takes time to develop the processes needed for success that allows the content to consistently go viral and make an impact.

The processes of success developed by Eli Knight has allowed the Knight Jiu-Jitsu YouTube Channel to be ranked well into the top twenty jiu-jitsu YouTube channels. The jiu-jitsu channel caters to well over thirty-thousand subscribers, and the videos have views that have exceeded two-million and counting. It's amazing what can be accomplished in life with an idea, work ethic, tenacity, and really good processes that are consistently followed, even if you live in a town as unknown as

Paducah, Kentucky. Eli Knight is living proof that passion combined with processes can lead to remarkable outcomes.

When Processes Are Stacked Upon Processes.

Having processes is critical to any element of success in life. Success is about micromanaging the process rather than the people involved with the process. That's the approach taken by Seth Daniels, a man who has permanently changed the competitive jiu-jitsu landscape for practitioners that are seeking to do the sport for more than just a hobby or a way to exercise.

Daniels created a promotion company called Fight To Win (Fight2Win) based out of Colorado. Daniels loves a few things in life; his family, grappling, jiu-jitsu, his friends, and what he is most known for, promoting events. Daniels was a very good high-school wrestler, practiced judo from a young age, and eventually fell in love with jiu-jitsu. He never made it as an elite fighter but found his calling in promotions.

Fight To Win is no doubt the busiest fan and fighter based promotions company in the jiu-jitsu industry. They travel the nation putting on about three events per month. That requires Daniels to be a road warrior, a jiu-jitsu gypsy of sorts. He has built a monster of a promotions company whereby each event has more than thirty matches.

The events have a rock concert look and feel to them backed by a working staff that authentically loves the sport of jiu-jitsu. Daniels was passionate about helping grow the sport of jiu-jitsu. He wants everyone to be able to train and live the jiu-jitsu lifestyle. His success comes from putting the focus on the fighters and helping them live their dream. The total payouts for salaries and bonuses to the fighters that are usually from the local area can exceed $45,000 per event. The 2017 goal for Fight To Win was to have athlete payouts exceed one million dollars, a remarkable feat.

How does Daniels pull off the volume of high quality events? He assembled excellent processes that were refined over time. Through trial and error, he created processes that allowed the production of each event to be turn-key operations. The stage, the lights, the videos, the equipment, and the music. All of the theatrical events are done no different than a concert promotion that travels from city to city with a skeletal crew of dedicated staff.

Human Software

It may be best to think of "principles" as the "what" to do in the pursuit of your personal goals and objectives. Principles are the fundamental truths that serve as the foundation for a system of belief or behavioral pattern. "Processes" are the series of actions or steps that are taken to achieve a particular end (mainly the principles that you are holding yourself accountable to). Think of it this way, "principles" are the "what to do" to live your life a certain way and the "processes" are the "how to do it."

Processes are like human software. Software programmers write code based on a sequence of instructions that should be executed. For software to work properly, all steps necessary to complete the task must be included, and the instructions must be in the correct sequence for the software to provide the right outcome.

Successful people in jiu-jitsu and in life organize their life around personal sets of instructions that become so engrained in their daily behaviors that they perform those tasks automatically without much thought.

A Legend And His Processes

Brazil has become well known for three physical activities; football (American soccer), Brazilian Jiu-Jitsu, and Capoeira. Capoeira is an Afro-Brazilian martial art that combines elements of fight, dance, acrobatics, and music. It is described as a game rather than a fight whereby two people perform quick and complex maneuvers that require tremendous amounts of power, speed, precision, coordination, and athleticism.

Rubens Charles Maciel was a very typical kid growing up in Sao Carlos Brazil. He started out playing Football, but once he was introduced to Capoeira and the related music, he spent his childhood practicing twice a day and seven days a week, eventually becoming exceptional at the art. But at the age of twenty-one, he was introduced to the sport of jiu-jitsu through a friend. While taking his first class and being dominated by an upper belt very easily, his energy and focus soon made the predictable switch away from Capoeira and towards Brazilian Jiu-Jitsu. What happened next was unbelievable.

Charles dedicated himself with the same passion and commitment that he had with Capoeira to his new love which was jiu-jitsu. He soon found himself training again twice a day and seven days a week but this time in the new endeavor of jiu-jitsu. As a young man, he would eventually move to Sao Paulo to train with what then was known as the famed "TT" Team after an invitation from Fernando Terere taking a huge leap of faith in his future with the sport of jiu-jitsu. He would spend his time living at the academy. He was jobless, broke, and away from his family and friends. But he had access to Terere for private lessons along with a long list of world class jiu-jitsu practitioners including Lucas Lepri, Eduardo Telles, and Andre Galvao that became his daily training partners.

Charles would earn his black belt in 2005, taking him only five years to reach that achievement. The quickness of his mastery is something that has been accomplished by very few people regardless of talents and physical abilities.

Once a black belt, the nickname of "Cobrinha" was permanently given to Charles. Cobrinha continued to dedicate himself to training and competing. He would win five IBJJF World Championships, four IBJJF No-Gi World Championships, capture the ADCC Championship an amazing three times, and was a multiple time winner at IBJJF Pans and European Championships.

Cobrinha who moved to the United States in 2007 to teach at Alliance in Atlanta, Georgia under master Jacare Romero, has since moved to open his own academy in Los Angeles, California where his teaching abilities match his competitive abilities.

Cobrinha is to this day one of the most dominant practitioners in the sport of jiu-jitsu and submission grappling. He is worshiped by his fans, feared by his rivals, and loved by his students. Cobrinha is an intense, offensive attacking competitor capable of ambushing his opponent from almost any angle or any opportunity. He will forever be one of the greats.

What set Cobrinha apart from everybody else is his quest for perfection. His pursuit isn't just limited to the physical aspects of the art, it is also the mental aspect as well. He has built training processes that are the gold standard in his desire to get on top and stay on top of the sport.

Cobrinha's emphasis is always on the process of practice and the practice of process. It's there that he refines his processes, his training, and his technique. It's his attention to the finer points of jiu-jitsu where he demands himself to be as exacting as what he envisions in his mind. In his craft, he is always, "doing it again" going through rep after rep. He executes on the process of achievement.

Cobrinha is tough on himself. He has created a standard on how he wants to do things, and he has bought into that standard with one-hundred percent commitment. Whether you are doing Capoeira or jiu-jitsu or running an academy, you do it with the highest standards, with the processes to back up your principles.

Breaking down Cobrinha's remarkable accomplishments it becomes a little clearer to see his processes emerge. He practiced daily. He practiced multiple times daily with specific steps and actions. He practiced every day of the week. He did this month after month, year after year. Those practices weren't spent on holding down a training partner to earn an imaginary advantage point. He didn't worry about "winning" in practice as much as he focused on his job of competing at the highest level and improving every single technique that he was working on.

For Cobrinha, the thought process became an unconscious way of life. He had created order, steps, instructions for himself that took the guesswork out of his decisions. There were no daily deliberations on what he was to do. It was all about getting things right and trying to be perfect while going home every day with the internal pride and performance that was worthy of being the best.

Cobrinha is now passing on his knowledge and experience to a new generation of practitioners. He's dedicated to getting them to do it right. Life isn't all about relaxing and taking the easy way while making last minute decisions on what you are going to do today. Everything is attention to detail.

There are many times in life where progress is a slow process, but quitting won't ever speed it up. Successful people work on processes, rather than constantly focusing on the desired outcomes. Spending time focusing only on the desired outcomes rather than the processes required to get there is the equivalent of always staring at the scoreboard during the game rather than focusing on what is happening in the moment and how you could execute to the best of your abilities in the present. Designing processes effective for life is often about subtraction. It's about getting organized and placing emphasis on what really matters in your pursuit of goals and then throwing out the rest.

What is so beautiful about jiu-jitsu is that it is ultimately an exercise in problem solving under pressure. Life is full of problems. During your entire life, you are introduced to problems that you know little or nothing about. These problems just somehow land at your feet, and you must address them and deal with them.

On the mats, jiu-jitsu comes with a host of problems that you must solve. Sometimes it is how to get out from under side-control with an opponent who outweighs you by sixty pounds and is younger and stronger than you. That type of problem can make you feel overwhelmed and be quite a challenge. Life brings many challenges that must be addressed while you are dealing with a full workload, endless deadlines, and usually limited resources. This often makes you feel lost, confused, or helpless.

Learning skills to help you navigate unfamiliar territory becomes a very valuable asset on the road of life, in business, and in relationships. You learn how to feel comfortable with the unknown once you establish processes that can be followed to solve your problems. Jiu-jitsu is supposed to be a fun physical game or sport whereby you get to practice solving problems on the fly while under the pressure of being attacked by an opponent who is also trying to solve problems.

Learning how to develop processes and then implement process improvement is one of the best skills one could acquire on the mats and in life. Process improvement is the systematic examination and refinement of existing processes. When you think about it, everything is a process, from brushing your teeth at night to opening up your opponents closed guard. There are a series of action steps that can be followed to help you achieve your desired result. Sweeping your opponent is a process from eliminating a base, shifting his weight, and using a lever to topple them. Making a sale at work or rotating your tires are all processes as well.

It was Vince Lombardi, one of the most successful football coaches ever who stated, "Process isn't everything, it's the only thing." Processes can be refined to make our lives more efficient, more successful, and more enjoyable. Using terrible processes will end up wasting time, time that none of us have to waste if we are to accomplish big things in life. A personal life can quickly become bloated with waste which leads to ineffective, inefficient, and inflexible processes.

Your progress in jiu-jitsu will be regulated by your ability to learn processes. These are the steps needed to utilize a technique to solve a problem. Improving your personal processes will enable you to stay competitive and increase your responsiveness to other people that matter to you in life which would include your employer, customers, spouse, children, family, and friends.

The best place to start using processes and process improvement is in the areas that either you or others seem to be complaining about the most. Are you complaining about limited financial resources? Then you may need better wealth building processes. Is your spouse complaining about poor communication? Then you may need better communication processes. Are you seeking to improve your health? You may need better personal health processes that are to be implemented and practiced daily.

Whether you are an Eli Knight from Paducah, Kentucky working hard to educate and spread tips through online videos, Seth Daniels working hard to bring jiu-jitsu promotions to fighters and fans, or Cobrinha looking to dominate in competition, processes are the navigation system and roadmap to your destination. It is an essential tool in helping you solve your problems. The hardest part of making improvements to problem areas of your life is getting started and taking those first steps. Such is the case when assessing and analyzing your personal processes that you practice daily, even if you never gave much thought to your processes.

The value of constant personal process improvement is undeniable. This will require adapting to a new mindset where ongoing improvement becomes the normal course of action rather than having any one single improvement become the main event in your life.

Principle 7: Adaptability

"When something goes wrong in your life, just yell 'plot twist' and move on." – Unknown

You will often find that the universe works in strange and mysterious ways. The chance meetings with others. A coincidental moment that combines with changing trends. An idea that sparks a personal revelation. In 2006, the universe was working in strange and mysterious ways in Hilo, Hawaii. Keenan Kai-James Cornelius was rolling around on some mats with BJ Penn, a jiu-jitsu world champion nicknamed "The Prodigy" who would later go on to become a UFC MMA fighter, a UFC dual weight-class champion, and a UFC hall-of-famer.

Penn's neighbor was Tom Callos, a 6th degree black belt in Tae Kwon Do and an early student of Ralph and Cesar Gracie in jiu-jitsu. It was Callos that was an early influencer in the career of Penn. Callos happened to be the step-father of Keenan Cornelius, another practitioner that years later would often be described himself as "a prodigy."

To be more accurate, Cornelius was more of a phenomenon than a prodigy. A prodigy is one who is miraculously gifted with no clear explanation. Cornelius was more of a phenomenon because once he found jiu-jitsu, he was what could have been described as, "all-in" right from the young age of 14. But even though the young Cornelius was, "all-in" for jiu-jitsu, he was far from gifted or exceptionally talented from the start. He would have to work hard for his eventual accolades. They weren't handed to him by the jiu-jitsu Gods.

Cornelius, like Penn, would often relocate and move in the pursuit of jiu-jitsu knowledge and skill acquisition. Whereas Penn took the path to California and then Rio de Janeiro, Cornelius would take the journey to Maryland to focus one hundred percent of his energy on training and competing. Maryland was the home of Team Lloyd Irvin, a sanctuary for lost jiu-jitsu souls who were by far and large American born. Irwin allowed athletes who were dedicating their lives to the art of jiu-jitsu to stay rent free in a house that was set up for just that reason.

Living and training at Lloyd Irvin's academy at the time were a group of medal and podium chasers that were dedicating every waking hour to the pursuit of jiu-jitsu including DJ Jackson, JT Torres, and fellow Hawaiian Andre Brunovskis who had already trained with Cornelius back on the big island. The group would train multiple times a day beginning with a late morning hard session with a lot of active rolling. In the afternoon the group would do a drilling session with less physical stress on the body, and then they would regroup in the evenings around 8:30pm to complete another hard-sparring session that wouldn't often end until 10:00pm or well after. In-between the battles the time was used to eat, sleep, stretch, and watch film of jiu-jitsu techniques or competition matches.

Cornelius, like each of his teammates, developed their own unique style. They were encouraged and given the freedom to be creative based upon their own physical traits and skills by Irvin. Cornelius, a tall, lanky grappler with incredible hip flexibility, eventually became a wizard of the guard. He mastered the art of grips, lapel control, the berimbola roll, and leg drag.

Physically, Cornelius didn't look like much. He's tall with blonde hair and a very boyish and innocent face. He looked thin even if under his gi he was developing a solid muscular structure over what appeared to be nothing but a skeleton below his skin. He certainly didn't look the part of an elite athlete or dominant champion. If someone told you that he worked behind the counter at a local auto parts store, it wouldn't stretch the imagination to believe it.

Early in his jiu-jitsu journey, nothing stood out that would indicate that Cornelius was going to be anything special in the sport. He was just an obsessed kid who was a mat-rat. By 2012, Cornelius, a purple belt at the time, would begin putting it all together on the competition mats and won what is known as a grand-slam in jiu-jitsu, winning the trifecta of the Brazilian National Championships, the IBJJF Pans, and IBJJF Worlds. It was the beginning of something special for the creative and unique practitioner.

2013 would result in some big changes for Cornelius, who now was dominating the brown belt ranks winning the IBJJF European Championship, Pans, and Worlds in both gi and no-gi. A few of Irvin's students and teammates of Cornelius were accused of some serious misdeeds at the academy. It was a public relations nightmare filled with negative press and distraction for everybody at the academy. It was Cornelius and a couple of other top competitors who decided it was best to depart the organization and move onto a better training environment where they could continue to work and develop their craft.

Cornelius would find his way to San Diego, California to join Team Atos, headed by super coach Ramon Lemos, a black belt under famed practitioner Andre Pederneiras, and Andre Galvao, an exceptional competitor who brings an extraordinary competing pedigree in addition to superior coaching talents.

It would be Galvao who would award Cornelius his black belt on September 14th of 2013. Galvao is one of the greatest competitors to have ever blessed the sport of jiu-jitsu. If you are religious, then it would only be fair to conclude that Galvao is jiu-jitsu talent on loan from God. Galvao would capture divisional and absolute championships in just about everything there is to win including multiple IBJJF world championships, ADCC Championships, Pan Championships, UAEJJF World Pro, CBJJO World Cup Championships along with other super-fight victories.

Galvao is a religious and spiritual man. He's a friend, a mentor, a husband, a father, and a lighthouse for many lost in the dark sea of life. Galvao is no stranger to hard times, adversity, and personal challenges. Growing up in Brazil without much in the way of financial resources, Galvao would find sanctuary on the jiu-jitsu mats. Like others before him, he would travel the earth in search of new techniques, skilled training partners, and higher levels of competition.

Galvao would learn a lot about life at an early age through jiu-jitsu. Life brings you bad days, hard times, and endless difficulties. He is a man of faith, hope, and optimism. It is the challenges and problems that make you a better person. Days are never always sunny. You must learn how to learn so that you can adapt and overcome.

It was Jessica Hagedorn who wrote, "Adaptability is the simple secret to survival." That seems to be the personal creed of Galvao. Jiu-Jitsu is an axiom of life itself. When you are surrounded by practitioners like Cornelius, Galvao, and the other teammates and coaches at Atos, you are surrounded by people that are creative and anxious to adapt. They experiment with moves and then take it to the next level and make something new out of it. Then they refine it to make it work for themselves and their own physical abilities.

Bruce Lee was quoted as saying, "All fixed set patterns are incapable of adaptability or pliability. The truth is outside of all fixed patterns." Life isn't all about fixed patterns. The world changes. The game changes. The times evolve. Like life, jiu-jitsu is constantly growing and changing. It is infinite.

Today's jiu-jitsu is modern. It is evolving from its original roots. Into the future, jiu-jitsu will change and continue to evolve again. You must adapt your game always to these changes. New practitioners mean new skills. The game is about adapting and evolving. Evolutions exist.

Galvao is an enormous fan of evolutions in jiu-jitsu and in life. He respects all the various fighting styles and how competitors develop and execute game plans to win. Some competitors can figure out better ways to win. There will always be those who complain about how somebody else won. In jiu-jitsu, they may complain about a competitor pulling guard, or doing the 50/50 guard. But the game is always evolving. Rule sets and competitions evolve. To Galvao, everything is useful in the right context or situation.

"Intelligence is the ability to adapt to change" – Stephen Hawking

The word "kaizen" is used in Japan to describe a state of constant and never-ending improvement. Adapted by businessmen, it stemmed from the age-old philosophy of warriors. High-achievers, in sport and life, are committed to constant improvement and adapting to change. If you want to be more successful, you must learn to change and adapt.

In today's fast paced world, a person must be open to adaptation just to keep up with the rapid pace of the changes around them. New technologies are being developed at a blistering speed. New processes are employed. Companies implement new methodologies to compete against one another faster and cheaper.

Adaptability is, therefore, a requirement necessary to survive. But to thrive, as successful people do, the rate of adaptability must be increased to stay ahead of the competition. One of the biggest breakthroughs in personal development occurs when you learn how to use the principle of adaptability to its fullest extent.

Adaptability has two sides to it. The first side is the conscious side. It's the side that takes individual effort, mental focus, and intention. It's forcing yourself to improve your skills, change your behavior, or better yourself in some facet of life. Adaptability works best with small, manageable steps that when consistently done builds momentum.

Adaptability requires you to embrace the change. You need to welcome the opportunity to not only keep up but stay ahead of the ever-changing world. Recognizing that change is inevitable reduces the stress associated with the change because you come to expect and welcome the uncertainties with a more positive mindset. Everything around you and within you is constantly changing. Your cells inside your body are changing. The earth is changing. Technologies are changing, businesses are changing, people are changing, and yes, jiu-jitsu and the jiu-jitsu industry is changing too.

The second side of change is having faith and confidence that over time, the human body and mind are quite adaptable to environmental changes that don't take the same amounts of conscious effort to make adaptations. The body adapts subconsciously without thought or effort. Eskimos in the Artic don't sit around all day and complain about how cold it is. They don't even think about it. Why is that? Because they have adapted to their environment. The human body can adapt to many things, both good and bad, so beware of what habits and environment you create for yourself.

If you feed yourself low quality junk food, your body will adapt to that food, and you will begin to crave the fats and sugars in the junk food. If you start smoking cigarettes, your body will adapt to breathing in the toxic smoke and nicotine. If you live in a co-dependent relationship with plenty of negative communication dynamics and fighting, guess what? You will adapt to that situation.

You should note one additional caveat to human adaptability that is important. Not only is the human body capable of adapting to changes and new stimuli, but it will also require greater amounts of that stimuli to get the same trigger response. Take for example exercise. If you have never run before, you may only be able to go out and jog a quarter of a mile before experiencing exhaustion. But keep at it, and your body adapts. It will be able to not only run further than a quarter mile, but it will adapt so that it can run at a faster pace.

The same holds true in weightlifting. That is the entire principle of growing muscle intentionally. By lifting weights, you are breaking down the muscle fibers forcing them to adapt by rebuilding bigger and stronger. Your muscles respond accordingly. This is the training effect in action. Athletes looking for improvement know that they can trigger changes within themselves by forcing the body to adapt to increased physical workloads.

When you first started to participate in jiu-jitsu, you probably struggled to last a full five-minute round of rolling. Then over time, you can handle two or three rounds of rolling twice a week. Then you can train three or four times a week and keep increasing the physical workload. That is adaptability in action. Top jiu-jitsu practitioners can train multiple times a day and seven days a week. They have adapted to their environment.

Through adaptability, your brain and body can make enormous changes. You can adapt to craving fruits and vegetables, adapt to strenuous exercise, build a faster and smarter brain, and learn all kinds of new skills.

You are also capable of embracing the downsides of adaptability. You can adapt to sitting on the couch all night. If you start drinking alcohol, you will teach your body to adapt so that it needs not two but three drinks to get a buzz going. Then four drinks, then five drinks. You can adapt to smoking two packs of cigarettes a day. You can adapt to where it takes increasing amounts of heroin or cocaine to get high. Why? The body adapts.

The Irish playwright and political activist George Bernard Shaw once wrote, "Those who cannot change their minds, cannot change anything." That was true in the 1800's, it is still true today, and it will be true tomorrow. The successful person will self-reflect and ask themselves, "Where do I need to grow?"

As the change occurs around you, you can either cooperate with it and learn how to utilize it to your advantage, or you can resist the changes, complain about the changes, and eventually get run over by them. It is a personal choice. Choose wisely.

When you embrace the changes, you use the power of adaptability to your fullest potential in the same way BJ Penn, Keenan Cornelius, and Andre Galvao did. Each of these practitioners looked for ways to use new changes to make their lives richer, easier, and more fulfilling. Their lives got better through self-imposed change.

Many of the changes that they had to make were hard personal changes that required the courage to deal with the uncertainty of the eventual but unknowable outcome. But they embraced the uncertainties as potential opportunities for personal betterment. Whether it was moving thousands of miles away from their homes, trying new techniques, or developing business opportunities, they did what champions do, they embraced the changes and let the principles of adaptability work in their favor.

"It is not the strongest of the species that survives, nor the most intelligent. It is the one that is most adaptable to change." – Charles Darwin

Principle 8: Minimize and Simplify

"That's been one of my mantras – focus and simplicity. Simple can be harder than complex: You have to work hard to get your thinking clean to make it simple. But it's worth it in the end because once you get there, you can move mountains." – Steve Jobs

The household arguments were getting intense inside the family home. "You are going to college and will get a degree!" screamed his father. "But I want to do jiu-jitsu! That will be my career," Bernardo shouted back. It's easy to understand how loving parents want to guide their children towards conventional paths in life that include traditional careers. Most parents can't comprehend how jiu-jitsu can be a career. Most parents also spend a lot of time worrying about how their children will be safe and secure in life as adults and how a proven career choice can aid in that pursuit of security.

Can you imagine how many times a conversation like this has happened between a young practitioner of jiu-jitsu and

91

their parents? Have you ever experienced the pressure of trying to follow your own path in life while pleasing your parents or trying to meet the expectations of others?

Bernardo Faria began doing jiu-jitsu at the age of 14. It didn't take long at all for him to become completely addicted to the sport. Two things were clear. First, Bernardo loved jiu-jitsu, and second, his parents loved him. They wanted what was best for him. They wanted him to have a good life that was better than their own life which is what every loving set of parents want for their children. The best path to a better life is often through a college education and a proven career profession.

Growing up in the town of Juiz de Fora about 100 miles north of Rio de Janeiro meant that most children in the area would have a high probability of gaining at least some initial exposure to jiu-jitsu. But living in a town in that part of the country of Brazil also guaranteed ample exposure to the economic realities of most major Brazilian cities. Faria's family grew up in what could be described as middle class. They weren't rich, but they certainly weren't poor. It's natural then to understand why parents would be concerned about making sure that their children would never end up poor or with a difficult life.

People young and old in Brazil were also aware of what life could be like in some parts of major cities in Brazil. Working in many lower-class jobs in a major city in Brazil often meant living in a favela. A favela is the Portuguese word to describe a slum. These are large sections of shacks that swallow entire parts of the city. Imagine an enormous and expansive neighborhood packed with one rickety shanty after another buried into the contours and elevations within the hills of Brazilian cities.

The first favela was built approximately 110 miles south of the family home of Bernardo Faria in the center of Rio de Janeiro in the late 19th century. It was hand built by soldiers who had nowhere to live following the Canudos War. The materials used to build these shanties include anything and everything salvaged or stolen from whatever source failed to defend their personal belongings. If somebody had a piece of wood or sheet metal and couldn't secure and protect it, that raw material became somebody else's living room wall in due time.

What most individuals in developed nations such as the United States and Europe don't really comprehend is the degree of variance between first world poverty and third world poverty. The favela's in the cities of Brazil are good examples of third world poverty. These are communities where the official police won't enter certain geographic boundaries. The communities are self-ruled which means that it's an entirely different food chain in the evolution of a society. If there happens to be some official police state governing the order and rules of the community, the police may be more criminal than what they were intended to regulate. The result of this social dynamic in these communities is that they are built upon the overriding principle of pure human desperation and survival at any cost.

If you are at all familiar with Maslow's Hierarchy of Needs, a theory in psychology proposed by Abraham Maslow in 1943 that is still utilized by professionals today, you will envision the triangle or pyramid that is typically used as a diagram. The pyramid portrays the psychological theory of human motivations which are based upon stages of growth in humans.

Maslow used a pyramid structure to describe the needs of humans with the more basic needs at the bottom of the pyramid and the most advanced needs at the top. At the bottom of the pyramid are physiological needs which would include core essentials such as air, water, food, sleep, clothing, and shelter. Next up the pyramid would be safety needs such as personal security, financial security, health, and well-being. Continuing up the pyramid would introduce higher levels of human needs such as social belonging, esteem, self-actualization, and finally self-transcendence.

When you live in a favela, about 99.9% of your time is focused on the pursuit of food, clothing, shelter, and personal security. Kids turn to drugs for either economic opportunities to survive or psychological escapes from reality. Adults are exposed to the most heinous forms of crime daily. When people think of crime in poverty areas of first world countries they might imagine their wallet or watch being stolen. In a favela, the stolen watch off your wrist may be a bonus, but the primary intended target of the robbery might be your kidney or some other stolen organ or human trafficking crime. Everybody knows of somebody who was murdered when you live in a favela.

First-world poverty includes public schools, welfare checks, food stamps, and periodic opportunities to visit your local Wal-Mart and favorite fast-food restaurant. Third-world poverty is a situation that people in first-world countries either don't understand or choose to block out of their mind. Individuals in first-world poverty often complain about their social conditions while using a multiple hundred-dollar mobile device and access to WIFI. Those stuck in third-world poverty situations inside of favelas would consider poverty in first-world countries as a winning lottery ticket and a huge step up the social ladder. This isn't to diminish the human suffering that occurs in first-world poverty situations. It's to bring a sense of comparison as to how bad conditions could be in third-world poverty situations like those found in Brazilian favela's.

Bernardo's parents had three boys, with Bernardo being the youngest of the three. One of the boys became an engineer. The other became a doctor. But now the youngest was not following the advice and pleadings of his parents nor following in the footsteps of his older brothers who achieved traditional professional career success.

Bernardo was a good student. He was accepted to the public university which would allow him to attend classes from morning until 5:00pm. There was only one problem in Bernardo's eyes, and it was an enormous problem at that. Classes at the free but well-regarded public university would directly conflict with his ability to train and practice jiu-jitsu. The arguments and battles in the Faria home between the parents and their child became heated and endless. How could a boy ignore his parent's instructions, pass up a free college education, and risk a terrible future life all to roll around in sweaty gi's with boys who had an almost guaranteed horrible future? That doesn't make any sense whatsoever.

But the parents yielded to the passionate pleas of the desperate son who was struggling to figure out the path for his own life. Bernardo made a deal with his parents. He would transfer to a different school and follow through with obtaining a business degree from a college that had business classes from 7:00am until 11:00am. After 11:00am, Bernardo was able to turn his attention to the pursuit of jiu-jitsu for the remainder of his waking hours. One year into college, his grand bargain that was made with his parents was paying off. He earned his purple belt at the age of 19, and as a purple belt he would win the Brazilian National Cup and become a World Champion in the Absolute Division in the same year. Magic was starting to happen on the mats. The hard work that he was putting in after choosing to follow his own path was returning some dividends.

Eight years after starting his jiu-jitsu career, Bernardo Faria had knocked off some important foundational milestones. He would achieve his black belt in jiu-jitsu, and he would complete his college degree in business. He was now an adult that could make his own decisions in life. To no one's surprise, he would fully commit and choose jiu-jitsu for his future without any objections from his parents. The boy was now a man who was about to step out into the big world around him.

Bernardo would eventually move to Sao Paulo to train under the direction of famed Brazilian jiu-jitsu instructor Fabio Gurgel who was known as "The General" at Team Alliance. Now training next to multiple world champions at the highest levels of the sport, Bernardo would hone his skills as a craftsman that would eventually allow him to become one of the greats himself. He would go on to win multiple IBJJF World Championships, Pan American Championships, and European Championships in the heavyweight, super-heavyweight, and absolute divisions at the black belt rank.

What set Bernardo Faria apart from most other jiu-jitsu practitioners, including those at the highest levels of the sport is his desire to minimize and pursue simplicity in his core techniques. His approach was not to learn and try to use one thousand techniques during his matches. His approach was to know a handful of techniques so deeply and so thoroughly that once he obtained his preferred positions, nobody would be able to match his skills in those pre-defined areas. Once he established half-guard or deep half-guard position in a match, his opponents quickly found themselves at a disadvantage even though those are popular and often used techniques.

But nobody learned and used those techniques quite like Bernardo Faria. He was always using them, refining them, and mastering the nuances of options that his opponents could choose from when defending the positions. He knew his opponent's responses better than his opponents themselves.

Bernardo would use this same approach in business as an active partner in the digital content enterprises BJJ Fanatics and BJJ Superdeals. He focused his efforts on an industry and business sector that he was already familiar with (jiu-jitsu) and offered customers a service that is of tremendous value to them. This allowed Bernardo to accomplish his jiu-jitsu and career goals at the same time which was another remarkable feat.

Bruce Lee used to state, "I fear not the man who has practiced 10,000 kicks once, but I fear the man who has practiced one kick 10,000 times."

Life can quickly become the pursuit of 10,000 things if you don't pay attention to what is going on around you. It's the rare genius that can minimize and simplify the complex into something magically clear and concise. It's the person who can master something functional and usable that achieves success.

Jiu-Jitsu is a wonderful and artistic endeavor full of beauty and endless possibilities. The development of techniques is infinite. The sport is like its own expanding universe of stars and molecules that are combined to create energy and feed life itself. But those endless and infinite options and techniques can become paralyzing. The constant pursuit of technique accumulation can halt progress faster than a sprained ACL in the knee can.

Jiu-jitsu can often seem as if it is a never-ending paradox. On the one hand, you have practitioners who are revolutionizing and moving the sport forward with the development and refinement of new techniques and positions. Examples of this would be advancements in new guards like the Rubber Guard developed by Eddie Bravo or the leg entanglement systems used by the Danaher Death Squad under the tutelage of John Danaher at the Renzo Gracie Academy in New York.

On the other hand, you have practitioners who have mastered very basic fundamental positions at the highest levels such as Bernardo Faria or Roger Gracie. Roger Gracie is one of the greatest competitors of all time. He is a 14-time World champion, mixed martial arts competitor, and the direct grandson of Carlos Gracie, Sr.

Roger Gracie is like Bernardo Faria in his pursuit of minimizing and simplifying his life and his jiu-jitsu into the most essential elements of success. Fancy does not trump functional. Foundational principles are of the upmost importance.

In Portuguese, it is an "estrangulamento cruzado." In English, it is a "cross-collar choke." It is probably the very first choke any new jiu-jitsu practitioner learns and often on his first day of practice. The choke works with the arms of the attacker in front of their opponent's chest, holding on to the gi in a crossing frame whereby the hands are locking onto the gi up on the collar of the opponent near the neck. It is a very basic choke. It is taught to every single practitioner in jiu-jitsu.

Roger is the practitioner that could take this very elementary technique and use it against the very best in the world. In 2009 at the Mundials, Roger Gracie submitted all his opponents in both the super heavyweight and the absolute weight classes with a cross collar choke from the mount position. This is unheard of in competition. How could something so simple be this effective against the world greatest grapplers? But that is the power of minimizing and simplifying one's pursuit of excellence.

Less Often Results In More

In jiu-jitsu, in life, and in business, the results and increased productivity often come as a result of "doing less to obtain more." How many times have you found yourself in life completely buried in the pursuit of too many endeavors? Life requires managing and mastering certain skills and attributes that if done correctly, results in a better and more productive life. Hopefully, that productivity correlates to a happier life.

Jiu-Jitsu is just a synonym of life. On a macro scale, you must deal with relationships, time management, financial constraints, physical limitations, and the development of personal attributes. On a micro scale, it's learning through experience what works and what doesn't as quickly as possible so that you don't end up collecting one million unusable techniques that result in you getting smashed in side control for the rest of your life.

In their New York Times bestselling book, "The One Thing – The Surprisingly Simple Truth Behind Extraordinary Results," authors Gary Keller and Jay Papasan dive deep into why you really want "less" in life. You want fewer things to focus on, fewer distractions, fewer emails to respond to, and fewer meetings or inefficient uses of your time. The benefits of "less" is the acquisition of "more." You want more productivity, more results, more satisfaction, and more time to concentrate on what you deem important.

Life is about cutting through the clutter to achieve better results in less time. You will notice in life that many people can go an entire lifetime without ever really accomplishing anything. This doesn't equate to their intended purpose, which often is an intended life without stress. Rather, the lack of individual results can compound the stresses in life magnifying the realities of having too little resources to invest in too many attractive pursuits. Jiu-Jitsu is similar in that some practitioners are much better at cutting through the clutter of a million techniques and game-styles while learning what works for them on a personal level.

Simplifying your jiu-jitsu game is an approach that allows many to enjoy the fruits of their labors while overcoming that overwhelming feeling when they step onto the mats in training or in competition. Focusing on strategic and high productivity areas means using energy wisely. This can result in the feeling of having "more" energy since you aren't wasting what you have on too many things that aren't offering you a rate of return on your time, mental, or physical investment. Focusing on minimizing and simplifying your life is the pathway to staying on track on your desired journey.

"If you chase two rabbits, you will not catch either one." – Russian proverb

What Bernardo Faria and Roger Gracie both demonstrate is that extraordinary results are directly determined by how narrow you can make your focus. Neither practitioner made their personal lives overly complicated when they were aiming to be the very best jiu-jitsu practitioners in the world. They didn't pursue careers that meant long hours at the office. They didn't go out socializing four nights a week with friends. They didn't have complicated relationships, pursue nineteen different hobbies, and watch hours of television each day. They narrowed their focus to what was most important to them which was jiu-jitsu.

Once they minimized and simplified their lives towards the pursuit of jiu-jitsu, they again narrowed their focus while minimizing and simplifying once again. Neither one of them pursued the perfection of a million jiu-jitsu techniques. That's not to be confused with not developing a well-rounded understanding to the full-array of approaches to jiu-jitsu. Rather, it's just that they learned what would lead them to obtain the most productive results with the limited time that they had to spend on learning. None of us have more than twenty-four hours in a day. Many of those hours are spent on basic elements of human survival such as sleeping, eating, showering, and doing necessary chores to navigate life.

Minimizing and simplifying your life is a rudimentary approach to achieving extraordinary results, and it works. Successes in life leave clues for those willing to search for them. If you look closely at successful people, they have common denominators amongst them. Sure, they all have well documented work ethic and dedication. But one of their secrets to success is their ability to concentrate on one thing at a time allowing them to advance in their skill development and area of focus.

"You can do anything you want in life, but you can't do everything" - Unknown

Principle 9: Tracking and Benchmarking

"All good to great companies began the process of finding a path to greatness by confronting the brutal facts about the reality of their business. When you start with an honest and diligent effort to determine the truth of your situation, the right decisions often become self-evident." – Jim Collins, author of the best-selling business book, "From Good To Great."

A parent will often become very proud of their child if they discovered that their child is visiting the library to read books, learn, and take the self-initiative to enhance their own personal development. It's a precious and rare moment when the parents get to sit back and think to themselves, "Maybe we are doing something right?"

With younger kids, it's a balance of guiding them towards productive learning versus letting them enjoy the imaginative phases of being a kid and exploring the fun and fascinating things about our world. For a child, everything is fresh with brand-new discoveries. Those early phases of life allow children the latitude to dream about their own future even if at times they are pretending to be a garbage man working the back of a truck.

It's common for children to gravitate towards some very interesting future career options when you ask them what they want to be when they grow up. As maturity and realism set in as they age, they fortunately gravitate to more productive career choices than cowboys and princesses. But what do you do with a child that is stubborn and absolutely determined to grow up to be a ninja?

What do you do when your little third or fourth grader keeps going to the library to check out all the karate and Taekwondo books so that he could practice the moves in his bedroom on his own? The most common reaction from a parent would be to put the child in some karate or judo classes and assume it's all just a phase that will diminish once something else catches their attention like cartoons or catching frogs the following month.

But that wasn't what was happening to a young Jason Scully. Everything just kept coming back to becoming a ninja. Unlike other kids who moved past becoming a superhero as a career choice, Scully never seemed to comprehend that being a ninja wasn't a likely professional path in the United States. Apparently, young Scully never scanned any of the employment listings after school or spoke to his guidance counselor to see if "Professional Ninja" was ever listed as a desired talent by a local employer.

Scully grew up with five brothers and two sisters. Money was tight for a large blue-collar family living in New Jersey.

They thought his obsession was just a cute little fad, but when his parents pulled him out of martial arts classes over the cost of instruction, he didn't lose interest or focus. Scully would look for ways around his obstacles. By the age of 20, he would obtain a job allowing him to earn his own money to be spent however he wanted to spend it. Whereas the other kids were getting jobs to buy nicer clothes, music, and to go out on dates, it shouldn't be of any surprise that Scully spent his hard-earned money on the tools of his future trade as an aspiring ninja. This would include all the prerequisites such as nun-chucks, a bow-staff, blow dart guns, hand claws that would aid in climbing trees and walls for stealth attacks from above, and Escrima sticks (which are the weapons used for Filipino stick fighting). When Scully said he wanted to be a ninja, he was not only serious but personally committed and diligent to his assumed future job requirements.

You must wonder how this struggle was working out for him in his own mind. This is a first-class example of man versus society and social norms. Did the kid really envision handing somebody a business card that had his full name typed in 36-point Franklin-Gothic-Heavy font on semi-gloss paper with the job title underneath that simply read, "Ninja"? Was he going to man his own business phone to screen for independent jobs, "Hello…Jason Scully professional ninja speaking…what kind of problem can I help you with today sir?" "Ok, so you're having problems with your neighbor. I can solve that with a stealth attack on Wednesday night. Is there possibly a tree nearby a bedroom window that could be used for entrance into the house in the middle of the night? Don't worry, I have my own hand and foot claws. Yes…we are bonded and insured…Yes, we work very discreetly and stealth like...Yes, we are rated by the Better Business Bureau...Did you see our testimonials and reviews on Google?"

Scully would one day reach a monumental moment in life. He discovered a ninjutsu school nearby that was teaching a curriculum. "Pay dirt!" he thought to himself. "Everything is coming together as planned. Now all I have to do is go to ninja school, and I'll be all set!" Showing up to that first class was exciting. He was bubbling over with anticipation. It was what he was waiting for his entire life, a chance to learn actual skills that would allow him to become a ninja.

Scully walked through the doors of the ninjutsu school as if he was passing through the gates of heaven. "What skills would they cover in class today?" thought Scully. The initial class was focused on hand striking. It wasn't on weapons, or stealth attacks, or secrets of the ancient ninjas. The class was teaching striking that required the students to conform to a stance that was more like a crazy yoga pose. It immediately became clear to Scully that something was wrong. He did enough boxing and fighting with his brothers and others at the bus stop to know that this wasn't practical in a real fight. In a real fight, you must keep your hands up, move your feet, move your head, and mix offense with defense.

Young Scully was now temporarily demoralized and befuddled. How could this happen? How could his dreams of becoming a ninja be so close and now so far? How could this ninjutsu school be such a fraud and filled with nonsense? Nobody even whipped a throwing star at a dart board, twirled nunchucks like a majorette spinning a batton at a halftime show, or anything practical at the class. It was a complete buzzkill.

Scully didn't fold up and crumble. He doubled down on his plan and quickly drew up a hasty Plan B. Scully would immediately return home to do the next best practical thing a young man with initiative could think of. He Googled, "What is the best martial art ever created?" A website link appeared that was for Gracie Jiu-Jitsu and he read everything he could about why Gracie Jiu-Jitsu was the best martial art ever. It described how Royce Gracie won the initial UFC tournament, and how the Gracie family used to be challenged by others in real fights and accept the fights as real proof that jiu-jitsu is the most effective art for fighting.

It's probable that it was destiny all along. The road to your dreams is always a long and winding one full of obstacles and detours. It was no different for young Scully who now had discovered an avenue to pursue jiu-jitsu. You could say that the rest is history, perhaps even destiny.

Scully is not a big man. Nor is he an athletic superstar gifted with any of the requisite genetics of a professional athlete. However, lacking the physical gifts of bigger and stronger athletes is what cemented his addiction to the art craved by others of similar stature. The thought of a smaller person being able to defend and win against a bigger and stronger opponent is very appealing to those who crave or dream about having the abilities to defend and attack if one found themselves in a physical altercation. Jiu-jitsu was now becoming the most important activity for the young man from New Jersey who dreamed of fulfilling his destiny of becoming a ninja.

History has a funny way of unraveling or creating mysteries. How did the big bang start? How did Newton figure out gravity as a force on earth? How did Jason Scully go on to be one of the biggest influencers in the jiu-jitsu industry? The answer is timing. Many things come down to just pure timing.

In 2006 forces were colliding. On the one hand, you had Jason Scully, an aspiring blue belt in the fringe sport of jiu-jitsu that was quickly gaining traction across the globe. On another hand, on the other side of the country, you had some young technical computer nerds that refined a technology platform that became YouTube on this new thing called the internet which wasn't yet fully being used by the general population. The technology and coding weren't as sophisticated back then. Forums were being used as advanced platforms where people from all over the world could conduct conversations and discussions about just about anything of similar interest (or more likely argue and berate total strangers anonymously and endlessly from the other side of the world.)

Scully has two dominant habits that often lead to extremely high success rates in life. First, he isn't afraid to try new things and keep trying and refining in the face of initial failure. That bodes well for most things in life but especially for technology and jiu-jitsu. Second, he is fanatical about tracking, documenting, benchmarking, and journaling his experiences which aid him in his refinement of intended purpose.

When someone asked a question on an internet thread about what options there were for the closed guard position, Scully did what he thought was the best way to communicate the answer. He set up a video camera and quickly went through the options that he used in his own jiu-jitsu game. He posted the video on YouTube for others to watch and learn from. The results and feedback were phenomenal. Suddenly anybody from around the world could learn tricks and techniques that could be applied to their own jiu-jitsu game and strategy.

Fast forward five years, and by 2011 Scully had a proven recipe and format for video success. It was refined, deliberate, calibrated, and repeatable. His videos went from 1,500 subscribers to over 80,000 subscribers within a four-year period. By then, the fanatical practitioner in jiu-jitsu was a bronze medalist as a brown belt in the World Championships and a bronze medalist as a black belt in the no-gi Pans Championships.

Scully wasn't done yet with his ambitions and dreams. He visualized a membership site that would allow him to share in detail the nuances of grappling techniques used by a wide variety of high level black belts. This led to the creation of his masterpiece and wildly successful membership website that is enjoyed by tens of thousands worldwide that is called, "The Grapplers Guide." The Grapplers Guide is a valuable resource for educational content that allows those who are not receiving the individualized level of instruction that they need from their local training academy and instructors.

The Grapplers Guide became one of the very first paid membership sites in the grappling industry which went on to become a major entrepreneurial success for the aspiring ninja-wanna-be. He wasn't quite a real-life ninja, but he was living the life of his dreams with a combination of his passion for jiu-jitsu and his quest for an independent career that didn't require him to work a traditional job under an employer.

Counting Things And Making Things Count

In the number one Wall Street Journal best-selling business book, "The 4 Disciplines of Execution," authors Chris McChesney, Jim Huling, and New York Times best-selling author Sean Covey created a simple, repeatable, and proven formula for executing on your most important strategic priorities amid the whirlwind called life. The four disciplines are:

1. Focusing on the wildly important
2. Acting on lead measures
3. Keeping a compelling scoreboard
4. Creating a cadence of accountability

Successful people in a variety of endeavors can produce breakthroughs and remarkable results by following proven principles and practices that have been tested and refined by thousands of individuals and organizations over many years.

The third discipline described in the book is to make sure you always know the score so that you aren't fooling yourself on your progress and achievement (or lack thereof). This is a discipline of personal engagement. Successful people play differently than others because they keep score with themselves against benchmarks that mean something to them and that they personally control.

It doesn't stop at having a mental image or visualization of what you are trying to accomplish. It takes it much further. It requires writing down specifically what it is you are trying to achieve, what are the inputs of success, and how you measure your progress along the way. By writing things down, it creates a visual and undisputable scoreboard on where you need to be and where you are right now along that path to success. There isn't any guesswork at that point.

Scully intuitively knew this and refined it through personal study and learning. Scully was a huge note-taker. Throughout his journey, Scully would write down what he was good at, what he wasn't good at, what his strengths were and what his weaknesses were. From there he would write down and dissect different positions like guard, half-guard, mount, and he would write down what he would like to do and what was preventing him from executing certain positions and techniques.

Scully was constantly tracking his progressions under the premise that if you write things down, track your progress, and benchmark your incremental goals and objectives, your goals were almost a certainty if you didn't quit. This habit and behavior also allowed Scully to remember what his objectives were for a specific class, or for a specific week or training cycle. Nothing was random or left up in the hands of others such as his instructors. He was holding himself accountable to his own goals and objectives and documenting the process along the way.

What the research indicates is clear. People play differently when the score is being kept. More specifically, people play differently when THEY are keeping score on themselves. When you can see the score, your level of play rises, not only because you can see what you are specifically working on and if progress is being made, but also what adjustments are needed. You are doing this because you want to win, not just in jiu-jitsu, but in business and in life.

Once you understand what it is that you are trying to accomplish, and you commit yourself to tracking, benchmarking, and journaling your progress (and failures), all that remains is doing the actual work that is needed to succeed. That's often easier said than done and we've all experienced episodes in life where we get excited about something and dream about achieving a big goal. We start the pursuit with enthusiasm and reckless abandonment before fizzling out and never finishing.

In the book, "Do The Work," best-selling author Steven Pressfield who also wrote "The War of Art" and "Turning Pro," shows readers that it's not about better ideas, it's about actually doing the work. This applies to jiu-jitsu tremendously because so many practitioners believe that the key to success is to just learn one more technique or trick from a YouTube video or mimic a move from high-level competition footage. Those are both excellent resources and useful tools, but there is no substitution for the tools that help you take action and successfully build and refine your own techniques that could be used against a resisting opponent.

You aren't the first person in jiu-jitsu or in life to run up against predictable resistance points along the way. You aren't crazy. You aren't unique or all alone. You aren't the first person to run into road blocks and speed bumps. Doing the work along a documented stage-by-stage road map can be an incredibly valuable tool that takes you from one end of the journey to the other side.

What you will encounter along your journey is the exact same thing that Jason Scully encountered along his journey. He encountered resistance points along the way. These were episodes of fear, self-doubt, and uncertainty. But those did not stop him, nor should they stop you.

Tracking and benchmarking your own metrics will reap enormous results. How you track them is up to you. What part of your game are you working on right now? How long are you going to dedicate to that component of your game? Are you working on half guard and sweeps? What half-guard set ups and sweeps are you specifically going to work on and implement into your specific and individual game? How many times did you attempt these techniques in class today? How many times were they successful? How many times were they not successful? Why weren't they successful? What was the opponent doing to negate and resist your sequence of moves or techniques? How will you be better prepared with a follow up to that specific position? How do you even know if you are making progress or not on that specific key position in jiu-jitsu?

When you track and benchmark important items in your life, you have a much higher rate of success. This applies to personal finance as well. What happens if you track your money versus an approach where you have no idea what you are making and spending and accumulating? It can apply to weight loss and exercise. It can apply to accomplish projects at work or at home. It can apply to hobbies like playing the guitar or learning jiu-jitsu.

If you want breakthrough results and you want to reach the upper levels of success, follow the proven principles of success by tracking, benchmarking, and journaling your progress. It worked for Jason Scully, and it will work for you. You may not become an actual ninja, but you can create a very enjoyable and successful life for yourself that is full of pride, satisfaction, and personal fulfillment.

"When you have defined your mission, values, and attitudes in the context of leadership, influence, and excellence, you also need to conduct a personal audit, checking how aligned they are to your current leadership practices. Where necessary, begin to make adjustments." – Archibald Marwizi, - Making Success Deliberate

Principle 10: Continuous Deep Learning

"The capacity to learn is a gift; the ability to learn is a skill; the willingness to learn is a choice." – Brian Herbert

There is a term used in both professional and elite amateur sports which is called "talent parity." Talent parity arises from the fact that there are so many people around the world participating in a particular sporting activity and that the knowledge, skills, and training protocols are so well documented that it is very tough for anybody or any team to pull too far ahead of the competition before the competition adjusts and catches up. This leads to a situation where there are roughly equivalent levels of talent in competitions where the winner cannot be easily predicted ahead of time.

Jiu-Jitsu has grown so much as a sport over the past 20 years that it is extremely impressive for any one competitor to pull away from the pack and consistently win at the highest levels for any extended period of time. The sport is quickly arriving at the state of talent parity. However, as you know in sports, sometimes one athlete or team can and does pull away from the pack for a stretch of time before the remaining competition makes the adjustments and bridges the gap. For example, when a top competitor has a win rate of over 89% and that competitor is consistently going against the highest level of competitors, the math easily points to a reality that this competitor is one of the greatest of his generation. The athlete has clearly demonstrated the consistent ability to stay ahead of the competition and dominate.

Leandro Lo Pereira do Nascimento is better known by the shortened version of his name on the competition mats. On the mats and in the jiu-jitsu world, he is simply, Leandro Lo. Lo was a natural lightweight (76kg/168lbs) but continuously ventured into various weight classes above that to test his technique at the highest levels of competition at events such as the ADCC, Mundials, Pans, and World Championships ultimately winning world titles in three different weight categories (light, middle and medium heavy). He is a super-star in grappling and one of the best pound-for-pound grapplers in the world. Fans of his style admire him for his unique and dominating top and guard passing game where he appears to magically float above his opponents before crashing and smashing into perfect position on the way down.

Lo has what often appears to be an endless list of wins over the most recognized names in the sport of jiu-jitsu at all weight classes. He is a legend that earned that status the hard way, which was by beating the legends before him.

It was late in September of 2017 that a relatively unknown grappler would find himself in Espoo, Finland, about

15,000 kilometers away from his homelands of Melbourne, Australia. Craig Jones isn't a small man. He was competing in the 88kg division (under 193.6lbs) of the ADCC, the most prestigious tournament in professional grappling.

There is something unique about Jones, especially for an elite submission grappling specialist. He's unassuming even with a very muscular upper body, chiseled abs, and a tattoo covering the entire left side of his rib cage. Jones has a boyish look to him and is usually wearing a smirk on his face as if he is up to some mischief or a gag against one of his friends. He's the classmate that you want to skip out of school with or grab a beer and tell jokes to one another. He has a blonde brush cut haircut more fit for belonging in the royal navy, and you just get this sensation that he's the underdog wherever he shows up.

On the competition mats though, Jones is like a stealth missile. He's a camouflaged chameleon in a sport that is often dominated by tan Brazilians. He strikes out of nowhere. He moves like water around rocks. On this September 2017 night at the ADCC, the dark horse Jones, himself an IBJJF no-gi purple belt world champion, six-time Australian champion and the four-time Pan-Pacific champion would be matched up against none other than the legend Leandro Lo.

As the match began with heavy-metal music blaring in the background, kick drums thumping at a furious pace, and thousands of fans in attendance, the bare-chested Jones would immediately drop down onto his butt into a seated guard. Many fans of the sport watching from around the world would raise an eyebrow with the opening move of Jones. This was an interesting strategic choice when going against one of the premier guard passers in jiu-jitsu history like Leandro Lo.

In typical Craig Jones fashion, he moved around Lo like wind around a tree constantly hooking and grabbing at the legs and the feet of Lo. Less than 90 seconds into the match, Jones would have an extremely deep heel hook locked up and was torqueing it with all his might. Lo would have nothing to do with tapping out of the dangerous submission attempt even though it appeared that his left knee was being shredded apart like a barbequed pork shoulder after being slow roasted for 10 hours.

Lo would scramble out of the heel hook and would continue to scramble as he negated attack after attack from the stone-cold approach of Jones. There are times in sports where you hear about competitors being star struck when they first compete against a legend in their sport. The up-and-comer reverts back to being a fan and believing that they have no business competing against someone that they have always looked up to or admired. They end up losing from the distraction of touching an idol. This was not the scenario for the underdog that fans were witnessing. Somebody showed up ready and motivated to go for the win, and his name was Craig Jones.

Attacking the legs from below once again, it was Jones that surprised Lo. Rather than staying low to dig under the pressuring Lo, Jones popped up quickly sweeping Lo. An unexpected scramble ensued, and a rolling Jones took the back of Lo so quickly that Lo didn't even have the time, nor the awareness to protect his neck. Whereas Lo was willing to physically sacrifice a lower limb earlier in the match for the chance to escape, there was no such opportunity for escape once a fully locked in rear naked choke was secured. There are two main arteries that carry blood to the head through the neck that are known as the carotid arteries. If you cut off the supply of blood and needed oxygen to the brain, the entire physiological system shuts down. With both arteries now turned off and with no way to breath, Lo did the inevitable, he tapped to end the match.

Now with loud Guns N' Roses rock n' roll music screaming over the arena sound system, the hand was raised on a shirtless Aussie who would never again be an unknown underdog. A star was officially born.

A Scientifically Proven Way To Skip Ahead

When Kit Dale gets together with fellow Aussie Craig Jones, it is exactly like two classmates skipping out of math class to tell jokes and bust each other's chops. It's one hilarious insult and unrelenting verbal jab after another. That's not to say that they can't get down to serious business when it counts. Dale featured Jones on a Back-Take Masterclass digital instructional course produced by Dale's training company Kit Dale Training.

Dale did not grow up doing jiu-jitsu. Dale grew up in Australia and had a passion for Australian rules football where he suffered a serious knee injury between 2008 and 2009. What made Dale so unique was his ability to learn jiu-jitsu at an unprecedented pace. What was his secret? Dale looked at jiu-jitsu completely different than everybody else who came up the traditional ways of old school jiu-jitsu learning methodology which is usually grounded in drilling countless techniques until they eventually are pressed into muscle memory.

Dale hated to study endless techniques and was frustrated by how most people are taught and how they learn jiu-jitsu. He saw it as a hinderance and considered the approach as obsolete as industrial age education programs developed to groom factory workers. He is vocal in his opposition to these outdated learning methodologies.

Dale had no interest in learning hundreds of techniques and drilling them each 10,000 times. That approach would take decades to implement, which is often the time it takes most practitioners to obtain mastery of the art. Dale wanted to mentally break down the fundamental elements of a movement and learn from that. He wanted to understand the themes, formulas, and common denominators of success within those techniques. This allowed him to learn how to deal with the countless variables that present themselves in live sparring and competition.

For all the haters of his outspoken approach towards old-school jiu-jitsu learning methodologies, it's quite hard to argue with Kit Dale's success. He's an extremely high-level grappler and competitor. He's a two-time world-pro champion, a Pan Pacific champion, an Abu Dhabi pro winner, a Brazilian Nationals champion, and an ADCC qualifier. He was awarded his black belt in only four years. Say what you want, but his output and results are undeniable. He backs up what he preaches with his own personal testimonials and results to show for it.

One thing that may come as a surprise for many jiu-jitsu practitioners is that Dale's unique methods of learning aren't really that unique outside of the sport of jiu-jitsu. They are well proven through research and study at the highest levels of human performance. It was just that Dale was the first to really cross-pollinate those learning techniques in a sport that has been virtually indoctrinated with teaching methods that could only be described as a few decades behind other major sports.

In the book, "Mindset – The New Psychology of Success" by Carol Dweck, Ph.D., learning comes down to how students grapple with hard problems and how they cope. The fastest learners are those that cultivate growth through effort and challenges. They learn through trial and error, success, and failure. They don't view their struggles as failures, they view those trial and error struggles as learning.

That's the entire point of Kit Dale's methods. He never was interested in learning specific techniques that must be drilled endlessly to be effective down the road. He wanted to learn concepts that could be verified and proven through trial and error. It's about mind maps, formulas, and concepts rather than specific techniques because if the variables change, which is constantly the case in jiu-jitsu, the formulas and concepts still work. You begin to recognize themes, and you get faster at using those themes to your advantage. Those themes require the development of what is called "myelin" in your brain.

To understand the concept of human learning requires a bit of knowledge on biology. Myelin is a white-colored sheath or coating made of mostly fat and cholesterol that insulates a nerve cell. Myelin's main function is to insulate the neuron, protect the axon, and direct the nerve's impulse in the correct direction and destination.

Imagine your brain as a bunch of jumbled and interconnected wires. Uninsulated wires would just zap everything touching it sending chaotic signals in every direction. An insulated wire will keep the signal moving in the correct direction towards its intended destination in the nervous system. Myelin is the wonder component that allows your brain and nervous system to wire itself for learning and growth. Build more myelin, and you build better learning infrastructure within your brain.

Myelin is the critical element that wraps those nerve fibers like insulation making the signal stronger and faster by preventing the electrical impulses from escaping or leaking. Myelin is what is needed for motor control, coordination, cognitive ability, memory, intelligence, problem solving, reaction time, perception, and learning. That's basically the list of required essentials for jiu-jitsu success. Jiu-jitsu isn't a sport like powerlifting where success is based upon raw power. Jiu-jitsu requires a high level of cognitive ability. The saying is true, "Jiu-jitsu is like playing a game of physical chess."

Tapping into the learning mechanisms of the brain has been around for more than a decade. New York Times bestselling author Daniel Coyle documented the methods to grow talent by tapping into brain mechanisms including myelin in his book, "The Talent Code – Greatness Isn't Born. It's Grown. Here's How." Coyle drew on cutting-edge neurology and research which he gathered by studying talent hotbeds around the world. He identified three key elements that would allow an individual to fully develop their own unique gifts and optimize their performance in endeavors such as sports, music, art, math, or business.

One of the key elements of hyper learning is described as deep practice. Deep practice is what leads to skill development. Skill from a biological perspective is a cellular insulation that wraps neural circuits that are growing while responding to signals and stimulus. This is where Dale differentiated himself from his jiu-jitsu peers who endlessly and mindlessly spent countless hours drilling techniques. Deep practice allows one to increase skills up to ten times faster than conventional practice.

Deep practice is a method of learning that is geared toward struggle and failure. It's forcing yourself to hone your skills right at the edge of your ability, the place where you are likely to make mistakes. By constantly challenging yourself at the edges of your ability and learning through trial and error, you can fix the small mistakes as you progress. You force yourself to slow down, think about what went wrong, adjust, and make improvements on the very next attempt.

This is why deep learning through active trial and error results in a superior method of learning as compared to mindless drilling or learning through observation alone. Reading books or watching videos can provide valuable knowledge, but you will never master anything without the repeated attempts of physiologically doing the activity.

Deep learning is an accelerated method of progress that produces big and lasting results because it allows you to leverage your time building skills as efficiently as possible. It is through making mistakes that you build skills.

Dale would describe the benefits of deep learning as that of dance instruction. Imagine if you went to a dance school and they taught you a choreographed routine. You would do fine and look good right up until the song changes, and the music is different. Then you would really be screwed with no idea what to do. In cases like this, you really didn't learn to dance. You learned how to memorize moves that were very specific to a portion of a particular song. In jiu-jitsu, or business, or in life, it's the same thing. You want to learn the fundamental concepts that will allow you to dance when the variables change. You want to learn how to improvise and implement principles that could be used in a wide variety of situations.

Learning concepts rather than memorizing techniques is the harder path to take. The key takeaway is to learn by challenging yourself through trial and error and making mistakes while taking risks. That equates to organic learning which won't be based upon any one mechanical style nor based on some narrow-minded outdated ideology.

This is the reason targeted and mistake-focused practice is so effective in real world learning applications. The best way to build a good neuro-circuit is to fire and engage that neuro-circuit. Mistakes will be a byproduct of challenging yourself at the edges of your abilities. Then keep firing those circuits repeatedly building myelin. The struggle is a biological requirement for physical and mental improvement.

When a person is passionate about learning, they are more apt to be persistent in their pursuit of that activity. They will be more patient and engaged during that fascinating process of constant trial, error, failure, and re-trying. It is that patient persistence in trial and error that is the key ingredient to building talent in any endeavor. When your body builds myelin around circuits, it requires a lot of energy and time. If you don't love it, it's doubtful you will work hard enough, consistently enough, and persevere enough to be great at the endeavor.

These biological discoveries are critical for success in jiu-jitsu, business, music, art, and life. Each time you deeply practice you are installing additional circuitry. The struggle, setbacks, and failures are not optional, they are a requirement for accelerated learning. To get your skill circuit to fire at optimum levels, you must fire the circuit sub-optimally which is done by making mistakes. When you pay close attention to those mistakes, think about them, make mental adjustments, and try again, you are slowly teaching your circuits. You are building myelin which cannot be built by ideas or thoughts alone.

What Kit Dale is doing for jiu-jitsu is he is cross-pollinizing jiu-jitsu with proven and modern neurological research and backs that up with his own public record of success. If you want to increase the speed of your development, learn how to "practice deeply."

We know in life that everybody wants the shortcuts to success. Everybody wants to make progress easier, faster, and more efficiently. The way to achieve success and the way to achieve it with less time and less money is to first subscribe to the practice of continuous learning throughout your life. Commit yourself to constant knowledge acquisition.

The second component of this commitment towards learning and skill development is to understand that there really are more efficient ways of learning. The latest research in science is backing this up. We've seen it done with people in the arts, with people in business, and now we've seen examples in jiu-jitsu like Craig Jones and Kit Dale. There is something to be said for "learning how to learn," and for those that make that investment into the process of learning, the rewards are well worth the investment.

Principle 11: Workload and Stress

"Working hard for something we don't care about is called stress. Working hard for something we love is called passion." - Unknown

"I'm in shitty shape for this," said Rob Biernacki. It was August of 2017. It was summer in California, and he was training with Yuri Simoes. Yuri Simoes is arguably one of the best grapplers in the world who is known for his unrelenting ability to push himself beyond typical human physiological and mental limits during his peak training.

Biernacki can be described as a unique guy in the jiu-jitsu world which says something because jiu-jitsu is often a giant magnet that attracts characters that could be labeled as "most unique" to say the least. Biernacki can best be labeled as a self-created fanatical intellectual. He shows more than one sign of being towards the right end of the functioning autistic spectrum curve. He's quirky, outspoken, and steadfast in his gravitation towards anything that could be described as "facts."

Describing Biernacki could best be done by saying, "Imagine submission grappling meets the character Sheldon Cooper of the popular television show The Big Bang Theory." His way of coping while living on the piece of rock called Planet Earth is defaulting towards systems, science, and facts and has no patience for those that can't or won't make decisions around facts. Those that make decisions based on whims, emotions, and preferred beliefs just add to his growing list of things that make him roll his eyes and shake his fist in a futile display of frustration up towards the never-ending universe above him. Functioning autistics are frustrated souls because everybody else around them appears to behave in ways that make absolutely no sense at all.

Biernacki is a high-level and legitimate black belt and owner of Island Top Team, a jiu-jitsu academy in Vancouver, British Columbia, Canada. The academy is a business that doubles as his personal martial arts laboratory along with being a sanctuary away from the crazy people that populate the rest of the world around him.

Jiu-Jitsu is constantly evolving within various geographies and cultures and comes in many forms. There are many descriptions or phrases behind the techniques based on languages or practitioner slang. Whereas the famed and innovative practitioner Eddie Bravo would shout instructions to his students about techniques or positions using vernacular like the "electric chair" or "the truck," Biernacki thinks and communicates in terms of frames, fulcrums, levers, and alignment as if he were teaching a physics class to aspiring advanced placement science majors.

Biernacki is one of the influencers in the jiu-jitsu world that is out on the edge of the scientific aspect of the sport pushing the boundaries outwards. He's aware of how new the sport is in the scope of historical athletics. "The highly scientific methods of training haven't really been developed or adopted yet in jiu-jitsu," says Biernacki. "The sport is still dominated by practitioners who either don't or can't understand the science of sport." It's too confusing, too complicated, and too time consuming.

Nothing makes a guy like Biernacki shake his head in disbelief than hearing anything similar to the old saying, "Just train dude. It's just time on the mats." Such nonsense would encourage Biernacki to curse the same religious heavens that he doesn't believe in. These dogmatic belief statements are such simplistic counter-factual statements spoken by meat-head practitioners. Living and rolling amongst Cro-Magnons can be frustrating to a guy like Biernacki. At least he can laugh and has a sense of humor.

When it comes to the art, Biernacki is fervent at both acquiring and sharing best practices in his passion which is jiu-jitsu. He'll stop at nothing to jump on an airplane for an opportunity to train with Marcelo Garcia, Caio Terra, Eddie Cummings, or Rickson Gracie black belt and influencer Henry Akins.

Biernacki has teamed up on multiple occasions to produce and release instructional resources with Stephan Kesting including the masterpiece titled, "The Modern Leglock Formula." Kesting, also a high-level blackbelt in jiu-jitsu, is a long-time influencer and leader in the industry, not to mention an advanced practitioner of multiple martial arts out of British

Columbia, Canada. He's a very popular figure who runs educational websites under the Grapplearts domain. In addition to being a prolific writer and YouTube content creator, Kesting hosts a successful and long standing podcast series that centers around the grappling world called the Strenuous Life Podcast.

It was Biernacki's knowledge and conceptual frameworks of leglocks that would inspire both Kesting to produce the instructional content and motivate Yuri Simoes to invite Biernacki down as part of his training camp for the upcoming ADCC tournament in Finland later that season. Simoes, who trains under 12-time world champion Caio Terra, needed to elevate his knowledge in this area and drill the positions and defenses before competing in a few weeks against many elite grapplers who were known for their crafty and brutal leg attacks. Training with the very best guys in the world is one of the perks of the job for Biernacki.

What Seasoned Veterans Know About Workload

One commonality for both Kesting and Biernacki is that they are both well aware of the balance that must be struck between high level training along with managing yourself for longevity in sport and in life. As Kesting often says, "In training and athletics, it's not the years, it's the mileage and wear and tear. You can't just constantly break your body down without letting it heal and recover."

Everybody is limited by the hours in the day and the wear and tear on their body and mind. Biernacki, the ever fanatic about science and systems that are based on research and facts is a proponent of developing concepts during your jiu-jitsu development. These concepts in jiu-jitsu should apply to live rolling as much as possible while minimizing wear and tear on your body. Practitioners at Island Top Team just don't roll that hard at his academy. They only dial up the intensity before heading into competitions. As Connor McGregor, the multiple weight class MMA champion and UFC superstar says, "You want to upgrade the software without damaging the hardware."

Jiu-Jitsu, much like life, is about improving oneself over a long period of time as in years, rather than weeks or even months. It's a marathon, not a sprint. But that doesn't stop many from taking a sprint like approach to navigating various areas in their life rather than playing the long game. How many times have you heard of a student cramming for an exam rather than committing to a lifelong learning process? How many times do you hear of people pursuing fad and extreme diets rather than developing a sustainable healthy and balanced diet for longevity? How many times have you seen jiu-jitsu practitioners train as if they are competing for Abu Dhabi in three weeks with weightlifting, conditioning, and hard rolls every day of the week, all year long?

Then, it's inevitable, the burnout or injuries start to creep in. There is a paradox in extreme excellence. On the one hand, you have individuals who try, try, and try for short periods of time and never reach their goals before getting injured, breaking down, or burning out. On the other hand, you have incredible feats of human performance whether that is people swimming the Hawaiian Islands, running hundred-mile races in extreme heat, or doing fifty Ironman races in fifty days in fifty states.

(Doing fifty Ironman races in fifty days in fifty states has been done before by the Iron Cowboy, James Lawrence, a 39-year old triathlon coach and personal trainer in case you were wondering). The human body is certainly capable of accomplishing some amazing things.

Life, including jiu-jitsu, is about managing stress and workload. Workload can be defined by the volume of the work multiplied by the intensity of the work. Volume and intensity are at different ends of the proverbial seesaw. Through periodization and proper training protocols, the human body can adapt to incredible stressors (physically, mentally, and environmentally). Volume is the amount of time that the individual is exposed to the stressors. Intensity is the magnitude of the stressors applied to the individual. Volume and intensity is the yin and yang of quantity versus quality in training protocols. You can train volume, or you can train intensity, but when you combine the two simultaneously for extended periods of time, eventually bad things happen.

In their ground-breaking book, "Peak Performance: Elevate Your Game, Avoid Burnout, and Thrive with the New Science of Success," authors Brad Stulberg and Steve Magness dive into the principles that drive peak performance, regardless of the field or the task at hand. Whether someone is trying to qualify for the Olympics, break ground in mathematical theory, or craft an artistic masterpiece, many of the practices that lead to great success are the same. What is shown through their research is that there are common cognitive and neurochemical factors that drive performance in all domains.

Humans are capable of learning how to enhance their performance in a myriad of proven ways including optimally alternating between periods of intense work and rest, priming the body and mind for enhanced productivity, and developing and harnessing the power of a self-transcending purpose.

Regarding stress and workload, we again come to another paradox. What has been discovered through research and observation is that by doing something that shocks or causes pain and discomfort, an innate stress response is triggered. The human body adapts to each unique stressor, building up increased resistance. Stressors can produce highly desirable effects, even strengthening the area of the body that is under duress. That's basically the entire idea of muscle building. Apply physical force by lifting a heavy weight to break the muscle down creating micro-tears which causes a stress response. The body adapts to the resistance and builds it back up making it stronger and bigger than the previous state. Viola! Bigger and stronger muscles.

But there are limits to the amount of stress that a human can handle at any given time. If the amount of stress is too big or lasts too long, the body not only fails to adapt, but it breaks down resulting in injury. These injuries can be physical, mental, and emotional. The human body deteriorates as it becomes exhausted by the stress and begins to rebel. Rather than repairing and rebuilding to newer and stronger states, the body creates elevated inflammation levels, and the stress hormone cortisol begins to linger, eventually reaching toxic levels.

The human body has many systems that run simultaneously, one of which is the adrenal system. The adrenal system is mission control for fight or flight response, repair, or breakdown. Overworking the adrenal system results in sustained fatigue. When this level of sustained fatigue due to chronic stress reaches critical levels, it results in a myriad of health problems, which develop into physical, mental, emotional, or any combinations of those bodily problems.

Stress can be positive, even necessary for human growth to occur. It forces adaptations. But too much stress can be negative, eventually causing great harm and damage to the body. The effects of stress and whether they are positive or negative all come down to the dose applied which again can be described from a physical training perspective as the "workload." The workload is the combination of volume and intensity. Too little of either and you don't obtain the benefits of training and adaptation. Too much and all heck breaks loose, and you go backwards due to injury, breakdown, and burnout.

What Biernacki and Kesting have both figured out is that jiu-jitsu mastery is the result of long-term volume that can be enhanced through proper and safe learning protocols. That volume of training can be enhanced by instances of subjecting ourselves to increased even cautionary levels of intensity. But it's the long-term workload that counts. Too much intensity over extended and prolonged periods will result in increased probabilities of a shortened career in jiu-jitsu. A short career in anything means that you failed to reach the benefits of pursuing mastery (which is a lifetime endeavor that never ends).

While balancing workload and stress, competitive practitioners aren't diminishing the importance of conditioning. Nobody is saying that conditioning doesn't count or isn't important in competitive sports. It's just that conditioning should never be confused with the development of long-term technical proficiency.

The Science Behind Physiological Workload

Lucas Lepri is one of the most successful competitors in the history of the lightweight division. He is an IBJJF World Champion, a UAEJJF World Pro Champion, and has won many Brazilian and Pan American titles. He, like Caio Terra, the Mendes brothers, Cobrinha, or Bruno Malfacine, have all trained their conditioning and fitness before important competitions. Conditioning is just one element of the recipe along with rest, mental preparation, body composition, game-plan preparation, and most importantly of all, technical skill. If you take away the conditioning of any of these champions like Lucas Lepri, you are still left with highly skilled and technical practitioners who have mastered the art of jiu-jitsu. They will still be elite practitioners even in the offseason when their conditioning is not at competitive peak levels.

Conditioning is short-lived. It's fleeting. Peak conditioning is scientifically unsustainable. Elite athletes at the highest levels of sport know this. Athletes must "peak" for their most important athletic events, whether that be the Olympics, World Championships, or whatever their priority race or event of the competitive season is. Maintaining peak fitness throughout a lifetime of sport is not even close to physiologically possible. Yet, countless athletes don't understand how workload, stress, and conditioning all must be balanced and integrated with one another while pursuing technical proficiency within the sport.

A human can only maintain "peak workload" for short durations of time. Something must give way in either the volume or the intensity of training or injury, burnout, or breakdown occurs. On the other end of the spectrum, any situation where training decreases in workload from peak heights, the body adapts accordingly returning to more healthy and sustainable levels allowing the cortisol and adrenal system to balance itself out for self-preservation purposes.

Practitioners also need to understand the downside of injuries, burnout, and breakdowns. In a study by David Costill at Ball State University, competitive swimmers displayed big drops in oxidative ability after only 10 to 12 days of no-training. In fact, a person loses approximately 50 percent of the peak fitness they have developed when they do absolutely no training for 12 days. There are some adaptations that an athlete can keep for at least three months, namely the cardiovascular adaptations of heart size and muscle capillary density, but peak fitness is a temporary physiological state that can only be reached through periodization cycles in training.

In a study by Dr. Edward F. Coyle Ph.D. at the University of Texas at Austin, runners begin to detrain (lose their fitness) after 48 to 72 hours of no training, and from there it takes two days of retraining to regain the fitness lost for every single day of training skipped. That doesn't mean you should never rest (quite the contrary as rest allows the time necessary to rebuild systems stronger). But if you take extended periods of time off from training, it will take you a longer time to come back to your previous levels of fitness. Therefore, it is crucial to avoid injuries and burnout. Injuries and burnout mean extended periods of time off to heal and recover. This results in going backwards in your overall development compared to an approach that properly balances consistent workloads and purposeful stress.

In another study by Dr. Coyle, a group of highly trained runners (who ran 80 miles per week) and cyclists (who rode 250 miles per week) ceased training to study the results on their fitness. At first, their measured oxygen uptake scores declined rapidly. Then less so as time went on. The best-trained athletes lost the most fitness. The less-trained athletes lost less (as they had less to lose). After three months of no training, the results were clear, all were physically detrained with a loss of fitness.

The counter balance to this physical phenomenon is understanding periodization and consistency. It becomes important, even imperative to either stay injury free and avoid burnout so that large setbacks don't sabotage your long-term progress (or force you to quit permanently). Staying in top physical shape twelve months out of every year is not humanly possible. Enhancing your technical knowledge of sport, or business, or art is entirely possible with consistent exposure and ample amounts of healthy stress to force continued adaptations in the body and mind.

What you are trying to figure out in your life and in your jiu-jitsu is the appropriate amount of workload that you can handle in your personal life. Your ultimate potential will be contingent upon the workload that you are able to handle physically and mentally versus what you think you can handle while juggling everything else that is going on in your life such as work, family, kids, and other hobbies. That requires a consistent and long-term approach to allow continued adaptations to occur. Since you are limited to 168 hours in a week and 52 weeks in a year just like everybody else, you must choose where to apply your stressors that produce the optimal adaptations in your personal life.

Do you want to progress in jiu-jitsu faster? That requires more workload. But more workload in jiu-jitsu will require less workload in some other area of life. Maybe that is your career, or relationships, or other hobbies, or responsibilities. But you can only handle so much stress and workload before your body and mind begin to shut down and regress.

You can learn a lot from Rob Biernacki and Stephan Kesting by managing your workload to levels where you are progressing at an optimal rate for your long-term jiu-jitsu career. Injuries, burnout, and breakdowns are part of the process. You will need to know and learn where your limits are and it's only through trial and error that you will discover where your limits are during any particular phase of your life. But if you can consistently work on developing your technical knowledge of jiu-jitsu, you are destined to reach your long-term goals in sport and life.

Principle 12: Modeling

Model [mod-l]

noun – a standard or example for imitation or comparison

Every sports fan loves a David versus Goliath match-up. Through fate and destiny, a weaker, smaller, less-worthy underdog opponent finds themselves pitted against a monster of an adversary that is likely to crush the soul of the dreaming wanna-be. The crowd finds sympathy in their hearts for the underdog. They cheer accordingly in their support of the little guy and the attempt to win without getting murdered in a public spectacle.

It's 2005 at the ADCC, the Abu Dhabi Combat Club Submission Wrestling World Championship. Marcelo Garcia, a small bushy-haired grappler with a permanent smile on his face, walked out onto the mat opposite his opponent Ricco Rodriguez. Rodriguez was a very large man who competed in the ultra-heavy division. Rodriguez played the perfect Goliath.

Rodriguez was born in San Jose, California and raised in the projects of Paterson, New Jersey. Rodriguez, the half Puerto

Rican and half Mexican was no stranger to conflict or fighting. He was abused as a child and forced into physical altercations. He had a hard life and he put his aggression to good use in mixed martial arts where he fought in major organizations such as PRIDE Fighting in Japan along with the UFC in the United States, eventually becoming the UFC heavyweight champion.

But now it was this little smiling Brazilian who was standing across from the giant. Marcelo Garcia won his 77kg weight division bracket (169.4lbs) and was now competing in the absolute division in the opening round. If any spectator were asked about the obvious size difference, they would have blurted out, "It's at least a hundred pounds in weight and a foot in height."

Garcia looked to be trying to stay calm as they brought the two competitors out on the mats. He was on one side of the mats swinging his arms wildly back and forth as if he were a swimmer getting ready to step up on the starting blocks. His rash guard was a black long sleeve. It was tight and form fitting around his upper body, and it had his name spelled out along the chest in white letters. The form-fitting rash-guard that traced the boundaries of his upper body physique seemed to only highlight the smaller stature of Garcia to the fans in attendance.

As the two slapped hands to begin the match, Rodriguez had the look and confidence as if he won some sort of prize by drawing such a small opponent in the opening round of the absolute division. He was pawing at Garcia's head and gripping at his upper arms in an attempt to get control of his opponent while leaning over him to impose his physical dominance.

Little Marcelo went after it from the start. He attempted takedowns, guard pulls, and arm drags. About a minute and forty seconds into the match, a seated Marcelo Garcia would attempt an arm drag that he quickly converted to a single-leg when the larger opponent tried to disengage. For a split second, this created an alley to the backside of the giant which Marcelo secured as the crowd ooh'd and ahh'd in massive satisfaction. It was David attacking Goliath without fear or hesitation.

Now it was Marcelo climbing the back of the giant, making his way north to the neck region. The crowd is going mad, screaming, hollering, and losing their minds. Marcelo would make his way to the top of his opponent securing his now famous backpack position with both feet securing hooks around the waist of Rodriguez. They call his position the "backpack" because when secured on a giant, it looks like Garcia is nothing more than a backpack on a student stepping off a school bus to walk home for the day, books in tow.

Rodriguez looked up and around at the screaming crowd, now in a full frenzy and he simply walked clear across the mat to get closer to his coach seated in a chair on the corner of the competition mat. As the towering Rodriguez escaped the desperate attempts of Garcia to control his back and attack his neck, the crowd started to simmer. It was a valiant effort, and they enjoyed the chance to see an upset, albeit a short, and fleeting opportunity.

The match continued with Rodriguez appearing to be more focused on squashing his annoying opponent. Garcia was like a fly circling around a restaurant patron trying to eat a steak dinner in peace. Minutes passed, and Rodriguez was still figuring out how to put this little guy away once and for all. As the second period began, it would be Rodriguez who came out aggressive. He had enough and was now determined to smash his opponent and end the match. Shooting in for a back-trip takedown, Rodriguez would secure it and get on top while smothering the downed Marcelo Garcia. Garcia now looking like he is fatiguing from fending off the much larger opponent was working to free himself from underneath the dump truck that was parked on top of him.

Marcelo scrambled from the bottom, escaped, and came up into the full guard of Rodriguez. Full guard is still an attacking position for the bottom player where his back is on the mat, but he has full use of his arms and legs while keeping his opponent controlled by wrapping and securing his ankles around the back of the top man who is belly down.

As Rodriguez opened up his legs to attack, a scramble ensued, and while the two circled around each other, the smaller and quicker Garcia ran around the backside of the larger and clunkier Rodriguez. Garcia would jump up and secure his backpack position again as the crowd went wild in appreciation. Rodriguez started walking forward towards the center of the mat, carrying Garcia on his back as if he were giving a little kid free transportation around an amusement park. As Rodriguez arrived at the center, he quickly stopped and intentionally fell backwards with force, aiming to crush the unsuspecting Garcia who was glued to his back.

There was a loud thud as Rodriguez pancaked Garcia with the magnitude of a piano thrown out of a high-rise building and landing on the sidewalk below. The referee jumped in as clearly the wind was knocked out of Marcelo as he appeared to be injured. It was a legal move, but incredibly bad sportsmanship. The crowd was now booing and hissing as Garcia laid flat on the mat. Nobody was sure if he would be able to continue. It would be a bitter ending to a fantastic match up to this point.

Marcelo Garcia, now down on points, and recovering from a vicious slam, popped up and indicated that he wanted to continue. The referee reset the two, and it was an energetic and inspired Rodriguez who smelled blood. He clearly had the momentum in the fight.

As Rodriguez came in aggressively to finish off Garcia, Garcia would scramble one last time to create some space between him and Rodriguez. Shooting himself feet first beneath the hips of the standing giant, he threw his legs upwards while pushing with all his might bumping Rodriguez backwards to the mat. Seeing an opening, he would reach back towards the feet of Rodriguez and wrapped his arms around the right heel of the now seated Rodriguez. The submission technique was a heel hook, and Garcia was twisting the leg inwards with all of his might.

The giant was trapped. The crowd erupted as they could see what was happening. Rodriguez had a split-second decision to make. He could either try to escape or tap. If he tried to escape but failed, there was an extreme probability that his knee and ankle would ruin while the ligaments and tendons snapped away from the inner structure of the joints. He made his decision, and it was self-preservation. He tapped to the submission, and the crowd detonated into wild celebration.

This would turn out to be one of the most exciting matches for spectators in grappling history. Marcelo Garcia would at this instant become a household name in the global world of submission grappling. He etched his name in history as his coach lifted him off the mat and everyone in attendance stood on their feet and cheered. In a jiu-jitsu biblical sense, David had conquered Goliath once again.

Marcelo Garcia would go on to become an incredible grappling champion. He also went on to become a very high-level coach and instructor at his academy in New York City. What sets Garcia apart from many instructors is his ability to lay out his jiu-jitsu content in a way that his students can absorb and model themselves off his previous labors and painstaking efforts.

Modeling is a concept that allows oneself to observe, map, and duplicate the successful processes that underlie exceptional performance of some type. Modeling as a self-improvement technique became very popular and was initially utilized by the work of Richard Bandler and Charles Grinder's work in early Neuro-Linguistic Programming (NLP).

It was the Neuro-Linguistic Programming techniques that laid many of the foundations of the work of Anthony (Tony) Robbins, the ultra-successful self-help coach and author of numerous best-selling books. Robbins is the go-to guy of the ultra-rich and famous when they get stuck, hit a plateau, or can't seem to duplicate previous success. Robbins is very talented at learning about an individual and then understanding what that person was doing when they were at their peak performance. He wants to learn and understand what formula and processes were used to get to the top of their game.

You can go back to the early beginnings of Tony Robbins career and see the dramatic influence of modeling in his approach to successful living and coaching. His breakthrough book, "Unlimited Power" which was written over three decades ago (1986) starts out in the very opening section with the title, "The Modeling of Human Excellence."

Most people arrive at some state of being subconsciously. They never stop and think about all the little steps and procedures that went into arriving at that state of being. Modeling is about turning the unconscious behaviors into conscious thoughts and mapping out the formulas of success that could then be repeated by that person (or anybody for that matter).

Successful people are very effective at modeling processes and procedures of others that they want to emulate. Modeling at its core is about finding people who are extremely good at doing something that you want to do and then following the steps that they have already figured out on how to do that. It saves you from what you don't have in life, which is unlimited time.

Once you understand the concept and the power of modeling, you will begin to see examples of it all around you. You will see people that are experts at modeling. These are the people that seem to be good at everything they try while also learning at fast speeds. Successful people seem to be able to do the impossible. How do they do it? They model off proven processes and formulas and duplicate the efforts of others who have already figured out how to accomplish something that they deem important.

Using Modeling As A Tool For Success

If you look at an example such as Tim Ferriss, the ultra-popular podcaster and best-selling author, you see modeling in action. Tim is very good at learning things extremely quickly. By the time Tim Ferriss was in his late 30's, he was already a top podcaster, best-selling author, angel investor to Facebook, Twitter, Evernote, and Uber, entrepreneur, and content creator. Tim Ferriss also enjoys grappling and jiu-jitsu.

So how does Tim Ferriss approach the learning curve in jiu-jitsu to get ahead quickly? He uses modeling. As an example, Tim took the opportunity to spend five days at Marcelo Garcia's jiu-jitsu academy in New York City under the direction of Josh Waitzkin, the co-owner of the famed academy. His objective was to focus on just one area of success in jiu-jitsu which was the guillotine choke, the same choke that was utilized at the highest level of competition by Marcelo Garcia.

Rather than trying to re-invent the wheel or figure out all the various components on his own which would have been a very long and arduous process of trial and error, Ferriss did what he does best. He finds the best in the world at some endeavor and then dissects their process on that chosen endeavor. Ferriss understands the 80/20 rule. It's impossible to do everything that an expert does in the exact same way. But it is quite possible to learn the core things that they focus on that make up the majority of the difference in the success or failure of the endeavor.

To add, Ferriss takes it one step further. It's not just learning what to do. It's also learning, "what not to do" when learning something new at a fast pace. He wants to understand what makes people fail at learning or applying the processes of success so that he could do whatever necessary to avoid those mistakes which cost precious time and energy. This allows the student to take all the good, leave out all the bad, and focus on what matters.

To help Ferriss model the success factors quickly was Josh Waitzkin, an international chess champion that the movie "Searching For Bobby Fischer" was based on. Waitzkin is no stranger to modeling and learning things very quickly. In addition to being a world class chess champion, he was a world champion in the martial art Taiji Tui Shou (Taiji Push Hands), a practitioner of Aikido, a black belt in Brazilian Jiu-Jitsu under Marcelo Garcia, and the author of the book "The Art of Learning: An Inner Journey to Optimal Performance (2008)."

Together Waitzkin and Ferriss would take a deep-dive into one narrow focus of the jiu-jitsu world. Modeling isn't about the width and breath of an endeavor, it's about learning at a deep level with a focus on the details that matter. Modeling is about understanding what the desired end game is. Where is it that you want to go? What is it that you want to accomplish? Once you know the answer to that, you work backwards on the steps that it takes to allow you to arrive at the end game. Otherwise, you start out by putting all kinds of effort into acting and moving, but you lack the focus and understanding of where your final destination should be. This approach ends up wasting time (and often money).

The key to modeling is to learn principles of success that could be used in a variety of similar circumstances. This prevents you from having to learn countless techniques or strategies that would have to be changed or adapted to as the world around you evolves and is constantly changing. It keeps you adaptable in life and sport.

Modeling has been an effective tool of the successful for very long periods of time. The concept goes back thousands of years. It's been right under our noses our entire lives with some individuals learning how to master the concept while others go their entire lifetimes without ever recognizing its immense power to transform themselves.

Whether you are trying to excel on the grappling mats, in business, or in life, modeling is an extremely effective way to advance your skills in a time efficient manner. Successful people such as Josh Waitzkin, Tim Ferriss, Anthony Robbins, and Marcelo Garcia all understand and leverage the power of modeling in their own lives.

There is no sense in reinventing the wheel. Understand what it is you want to achieve in life. Whether you are trying to succeed in business, relationships, health, or jiu-jitsu, there are countless people that have already figured out how to do certain components of those skills extremely effective and thereby have become experts in their fields. Pick your models for success and emulate their processes.

Your life can often be judged by the company you keep. Pay attention to who you associate with and who you are trying to emulate. Surround yourself with positive influences and with people that have either done something that you want to accomplish, or they know how you can do it. Adapt yourself to the environment that is required for success in that endeavor. Modeling creates the environment in everything that you do to succeed.

Learn to model and learn how to obtain breakthrough performances in jiu-jitsu and in life.

Principle 13: Do Your Best

"Doing your best is more important than being the best." – Zig Ziglar

There's a calendar date in history that doesn't stand out for any particular reason any more than any other random day in history for most jiu-jitsu practitioners. The date is April the 23rd, 1910. Nobody reading this today was even alive on that date more than a century ago. It was a Saturday like any other day at the Sorbonne in Paris, France.

The Sorbonne is an institution and a stunningly beautiful building complex resembling a small downtown university campus that has been around since the 13th century. It is a center of intelligence, culture, and knowledge in both the sciences and the arts. It is what you would expect to see in Paris, France built with columns, massive stone, steeples, and grand architectural designs that have stood the test of time. Over the centuries it has stood for what it continues to stand for to this day, which is a promise of excellence.

On Saturday, April the 23rd in 1910 a speech was being delivered by Theodore Roosevelt, the former president of the United States from September 14, 1901, through March 3, 1909. Roosevelt was a pudgy intellect. A graduate from Harvard University who at only 5'9" tall weighed over 220lbs.

Before his second presidential election, Roosevelt needed to lose 20 pounds. He did what many of you would have done, he trained in judo and jiu-jitsu. Roosevelt trained the same type of judo and jiu-jitsu that the Gracies learned in Brazil from Mitsuyo Maeda and other Japanese practitioners. Roosevelt would seek the assistance of Yamashita Yoshiaki, the pioneer of judo in the United States and a direct student of Jigoro Kano, the official "founder" of Judo. This is the exact same judo that would go on to become an Olympic sport.

During the spring of 1904, Roosevelt practiced his judo, jiu-jitsu, wrestling, and boxing three afternoons a week in a ground floor office of the White House. His training partners included his sons, his private secretary, the Japanese naval attaché, Secretary of War William Howard Taft, and the Secretary of the Interior Gifford Pinchot.

But now within the confines of the Sorbonne, Roosevelt was delivering one of his greatest speeches that has stood the test of time. It was fitting that it was delivered at the Sorbonne, as now the words would last the centuries long after generations have passed into other worlds. The speech was entitled "Citizenship In A Republic," but the excerpt is now known as, "The Man In The Arena":

"It is not the critic who counts; not the man who points out how the strong man stumbles, or where the doer of deeds could have done them better. The credit belongs to the man who is actually in the arena, whose face is marred by dust and sweat and blood; who strives valiantly; who errs, who comes short again and again, because there is no effort without error and shortcoming; but who does actually strive to do the deeds; who knows great enthusiasms, the great devotions; who spends himself in a worthy cause; who at the best knows in the end the triumph of high achievement, and who at the worst, if he fails, at least fails while daring greatly, so that his place shall never be with those cold and timid souls who neither know victory nor defeat." – Theodore Roosevelt, April 23, 1910

Daring greatly. That's what you are asking yourself to do in your lifetime. That's what you are asking yourself to do in jiu-jitsu, in business, and in life. That's what you do if you ever walk out onto the competition mats and face your fears and battle the demons of uncertainty. That's the message to be passed on to your children and your children's children.

You will find yourself during your life in difficult places, in difficult times, in difficult positions. This will make you feel exposed, afraid, and insecure. Who are you to succeed? What gives you the right? You will be criticized, judged, and shunned during your efforts. You will be doubted.

You must overcome your fears and put yourself out there. You must show up and be seen. You must try when you are unsure if you have any chance to succeed. So, if you must try, you must try your best and dare greatly to exceed yourself. This is what it takes to break through the fear and the insecurities of not being enough or doing enough in life. There may never be "enough." There is only enough when you do your best and dare greatly.

What is it that in your life that is worth doing even if there is a chance of failure? What is it that you want to do knowing that uncertainties will always exist? And if you are going to do these deeds, will you do them to the best of your abilities? Will you give yourself every chance of success while sharing your talents with others?

If you are waiting to be hand-selected or randomly picked by some other person, you may be waiting for a long time. Possibly forever. If you are waiting for permission from some higher power or influential person to do your deeds, you may be waiting for a long time. Possibly forever. Never give the power of selection over to another man. Choose yourself. It's your life to live for yourself.

When you attempt your deeds in life, it will require two types of sweat. The first type of sweat will be from the physical labor as you toil and navigate the troubles and obstacles of your deeds. The second type of sweat will be from the cold sweat that grows from the fear of putting yourself out there in the arena when others will judge and criticize.

There is no way that you can attempt anything in life and not draw the attention of an onlooker or bystander that has their unsolicited two-cents to add to your endeavors and pursuits.

They may not even know you personally but may make very personal comments about you. They will judge you. They will sometimes be mean and vindictive. But you must not allow these bystanders to prevent you from your deeds. They must not stop you from doing your best and daring greatly.

Your deeds may not have anything to do with winning and losing in a competition. Your deeds are about winning or losing in your life and the journey ahead of you. Your deeds require you to show up, toil, labor, sweat, stumble, fail, fail again, and fail again. Show up, get up, stand up straight. Not because you must silence your critics but rather because you want to find that fulfillment within yourself as you do your deeds.

This is what must be done to be who you want to be. This is not about being what someone else wants you to be. For their own self-interest, they may very well want or hope that you become a failure. That will give them temporary comfort for their own shortcomings and inadequacies within their own life and pursuits. Show up, even though you know you will experience some beatdowns in life. You will experience countless beatdowns in jiu-jitsu practice. So what? Who cares? Show up, do your deeds, do your best, and dare greatly. Find the courage to jump into your own arena.

What you can never know for sure, is what your future holds. You can only put in the effort into your deeds, dare greatly, and see where the results of your hard work lead you. We see this repeatedly from examples all over the world.

On The Other Side Of The Planet

Nestled along the River Torrens and home to renowned museums, art galleries, and historical collections is the city of Adelaide in South Australia. When people think of Australian cities, they normally imagine Melbourne or Sydney, both on the southeastern coasts of the massive island parked in the Pacific Ocean.

To the west of the better-known metropolitan cities in Australia sits the coastal city of Adelaide. It's fitting to be in Australia and describe your location something expected as, "We are 100 kilometers to the northeast of Kangaroo Island." That's exactly what Tom Davey would say if asked where he is from. Davey is another jiu-jitsu practitioner who has carved out fans from around the world. He's an extremely likeable and encouraging jiu-jitsu instructor who benefited from the not-so-little technological invention called YouTube.

It's YouTube that hosts Davey's channel called, "The Grappling Academy." For those living in the west, Davey is clear on the other side of the planet, living in a city that geographically challenged westerners have never heard of. But when there is a will, there is a way. Not every nook and cranny on this earth is peppered with jiu-jitsu schools like those in New York City, Southern California, or the major cities in Brazil. If you think the commute to your academy is a little inconvenient, could you imagine having to travel to Texas in the United States from Australia to get exposure to your ranking instructor Carlos Machada? Carlos Machada is the eldest of the five Machado brothers, an 8th degree coral belt who started training jiu-jitsu at the age of 4 from his uncles Carlos and Helio Gracie and is the ranking instructor to Tom Davey.

But there was a will, and there was a way, albeit one that required Davey to dare greatly and get creative. The martial arts that were available locally were the traditional and common ones like karate and Jeet Kune Do. But there weren't options for those who wanted to pursue jiu-jitsu. That didn't stop Davey. He started his own academy South Coast BJJ & MMA. He wasn't a black belt. He wasn't a brown belt. He wasn't even a purple belt. That didn't stop Davey. He dared greatly. He ignored the critics. Davey would seek out the advice and counsel from John Will, one of Australian's "dirty dozen." It was John Will who was one of the pioneers of jiu-jitsu in Australia and one of the first twelve individuals to receive the ranking of jiu-jitsu black belt in Australia.

Now, years later and thousands of fans strong with countless video lessons uploaded on his YouTube Channel, Davey is an "overnight success." It was years of unpaid and unrewarded labor, struggles, obstacles, and logistical problems that he would have to overcome. But by daring greatly, he would introduce local students to jiu-jitsu, which also gave him a steady stream of willing training partners. They would all improve together. He created something out of nothing because he did his best.

A Role Model Arises From Nowhere

At the center of the jiu-jitsu universe is one single person. It's yourself. It's not the ghost of Helio Gracie or the recent absolute winner at the ADCC. Tomorrow, you will be slightly different partly because of jiu-jitsu, just like today you are slightly different than the person who stepped out on the mats yesterday, last month, and last year. That is the magic of jiu-jitsu.

During your journey, you will encounter people that will try to describe you, label you, or box you in as if you were being cast as a permanent character in a drama play. But that may not be the real you or the you that you become along the journey.

That's the case with Nick Albin. Nick didn't appear to be much different than any other young guy when doing his first jiu-jitsu competition. He had a white belt wrapped around his waist, his blue gi pants were far too long and curling under the back of his heels. He could mop the mats and grapple standup at the same time. Albin looked a bit uncertain in the surroundings of a jiu-jitsu competition, but he was certain of one thing; he liked to grapple.

Albin was just a big kid who liked to roughhouse. It was a way to clear his head, use his body, and make sense of a complex and confusing world. Over the years, the big kid disguised as a young man would continue to fill out physically, add a beard, add some muscle, and add some perspective on what everything means when you are trying to figure out what the world means in Louisville, Kentucky and beyond. "What am I supposed to do with myself? How am I supposed to fit in? How am I to support myself through work?" thought Albin on a daily basis.

Albin was a wrestler at heart which meant he loved physical movement, pressure, pushing the pace, and action. That sometimes meant that he wasn't the most pleasant of partners for others on the mat who may be trying to work a particular technique or just trying to survive a class while dead tired from everything happening to them in the big-bad-outside world. Depending on the day, jiu-jitsu can either be a sanctuary from your problems outside of the academy, or a pressure cooker that adds to your problems while you try to keep up physically with others inside the academy.

Between the full head of brown hair, the beard, the mustache, and the physical bulk that was added to his skeletal frame, a frustrated teammate lashed out during a training roll at Albin, referring to him as the Star Wars character Chewbacca. The training partner meant it as an insult, but from then on Albin would simply be known as, "Chewy." This insult was the gift that just keeps on giving, and now the pearls that he shares with the rest of the world on blogs, YouTube, and social media would be delivered from his moniker "ChewJitsu." The scoreboard is now Chewy "1", unknown frustrated training partner "0."

What is unique about Chewy (Albin) is his intellectual and philosophical depth that one wouldn't expect from a Chewbacca character that likes to rough-house and as they say in Kentucky, "rassle." Chewy allowed everyone around him and from around the world to watch him blossom and grow up in real time. Chewy's gift to the jiu-jitsu world was the authentic and raw truth of his personal metamorphosis brought on by the art of jiu-jitsu. You repeatedly hear how jiu-jitsu changes lives. Chewy is "exhibit A" on how jiu-jitsu changes lives.

It was his generous and honest sharing of his good days and bad, his personal victories and humbling losses, the promotions, the setbacks, the injuries, the frustrations, and his grace born from maturing with everybody watching, listening, and reading. Chewy was the guy who showed up on the mats and did his best. He was the writer that wasn't up for any Pulitzer prizes any time soon. His videos weren't going to be made into any Hollywood blockbuster films. But he shared his talents, did his best, and along the way he became one of the best teachers and role models in the jiu-jitsu community because he dared greatly and exceeded himself.

Practitioners didn't follow him because of his belt rank (although he is a very technical black belt). They didn't follow him because he had more philosophical knowledge and life insight than Plato or Aristotle. They didn't follow him because he had the jiu-jitsu record of Rickson Gracie or the reputation of John Danaher. They followed him because of his authentic, raw, and relatable insights that he generously shared while on the path to success. He's a gem amongst a pile of rocks.

Chewy teaches at Derby City Martial Arts in Louisville, Kentucky. That's not exactly a Mecca of the jiu-jitsu world. But Chewy learned how to become the center of his own universe by doing his best day after day, week after week, and year after year. He kept forging himself into somebody new the next day. Medals were won, MMA fights ended with his hand raised in victory, and belts were wrapped around his waist. But it was the person he became that enabled him to take home those medals, win those fights, and have belts wrapped around his waist that influenced so many around him and beyond his geographic location.

Jiu-jitsu is like a permanent cocoon that breeds the physical, mental, and emotional changes in oneself. You are inside the cocoon and outside the cocoon simultaneously. You appear to be fixed in character and abilities for the day yet are transforming yourself from the inside-out. Goals change, abilities change, ranks change. Your mind changes. Your body changes. Your experiences change. Your attitudes and perspective on things change. You change. You become new versions of you depending on the work and effort you put into becoming a greater version of yourself through jiu-jitsu.

What humanity all shares is the ability to forge ahead and change oneself. Those changes only come through toil, labor, failures, setbacks and overcoming obstacles. It requires one to do the deeds that must be done to accomplish the metamorphous you seek. Theodore Roosevelt, Tom Davey, and Nick Albin all had to navigate the personal changes required to move a step closer to the person that they wanted to become. They all did the deeds required for change. They all did their best and dared greatly without any assurances that the outcome would be guaranteed.

So too must you do the deeds, do your best, and dare greatly if you are to become the person that you want to become before your time is done.

Principle 14: Goals

"Setting goals is the first step in turning the invisible into the visible." – Tony Robbins

On a warm August Saturday night, a silhouette of a wide shoulder wrecking machine walked out onto a raised platform under the music, lights, and energy that were worthy of a professional wrestling event. Through the laser lights and fog, the physical spectacle of a V-shaped man walked across the mat for the Fight To Win Pro 44 event in Boston, Massachusetts. The event, live-streamed around the world, would display the skills and talents of Yuri Simoes, a two-time ADCC gold medalist, and IBJJF multiple time world champion.

Simoes is known for his incredible work ethic and tenacity on the training mats. A champion that earns every victory in competition by pushing himself to exhaustion with his training partners. Just when you think he's run out of gas, he seems to always have another reserve tank ready to switch to. He's an aggressive submission machine that could armbar any man not securing his outer limbs.

Simoes started training jiu-jitsu at the young age of 9 and would follow his grappling passion to become a nomadic warrior that would travel throughout Europe, Brazil, and the United States refining his combat skills against the very best opponents he could challenge.

Simoes would face-off against Travis Stevens, one of the most decorated athletes in grappling and martial arts. Stevens is a Renzo Gracie black belt in jiu-jitsu. What made Stevens special was the fact that jiu-jitsu was more of just a side hobby and add-on to his to his primary love which is judo. His jiu-jitsu pursuits began as a way to keep training when he was too injured to train judo throws. Stevens is a lifetime judoka and a great one at that. Stevens, a three-time Olympian, won Olympic silver at the 2016 Summer Olympics in Rio de Janeiro, Brazil against the best judo players in the world. This is an amazing feat of aptitude and ability considering how far behind the United States is in the realm of competitive judo around the globe.

When Stevens puts his mind to something, he goes after it with reckless abandonment. He's obsessed. He's passionate. He's focused. He's unrelenting. He's the type of athlete that trains day after day, week after week, year after year, working on the most minutia of details that could improve his techniques and skills.

Jiu-Jitsu, like many sports and physical activities, can increase the odds of an eventual orthopedic type of injury. But there is a difference with judo. Judo IS injuries. One cannot do judo at the highest levels of competition without getting injured. Herniated disks, sprained ligaments, dislocated joints, cauliflower ears, broken bones, torn tendons, concussions, infections, and muscles that seem to never stop aching are all things that Stevens dealt with at that level of competitive combat. When technical training was done, that just meant it was time to move on to strength training or program specific conditioning for Stevens. His life as a high-level athlete in martial arts was one that mandated training with and around constant injuries.

What drives Stevens to push himself to limits that would break most human beings? It's one simple answer; Goals. Stevens picks his goals and then develops and commits to the training necessary to reach those goals. That means competition goals, technique goals, conditioning goals, body composition goals, and time management goals. Stevens assembled goals that included the development of personal systems that were used not only in training but in competition. Stevens knew that matches are won and lost in the strategic decisions that an athlete must make during combat and during training. It comes down to developing a structure to teach oneself how to win, and Stevens obviously knew how to win at the highest level of international competition.

When it comes to winning and achieving his goals, Stevens never allows himself any crutches. There are no personal excuses. He takes full responsibility for his actions, his behaviors, and his results. He believes strongly in controlling your own destiny and to never allow others to impact or influence the choices that will take you off track.

Stevens has always followed a saying throughout his career, "If I can breathe, if I can walk, I can fight. If I can fight, I can win! I will never let anything get in my way of achieving my goals."

Stevens was coached in judo by Jimmy Pedro in Wakefield, Massachusetts, a northern suburb of Boston. Pedro himself has a stunning resume of accolades in judo including multiple Pan Am and World Championships. He is a three-time Olympian and two-time bronze medalist in both the 2004 Olympics in Athens, Greece and the 1996 Games in Atlanta, Georgia.

Stevens would often train judo at Pedro's school with another Boston martial artist by the name of Mike Zenga. Zenga, like Stevens, is another one of those rare breeds that possess black belts in judo and jiu-jitsu. But where Stevens was known for his international competition success, it was Zenga that often was the quiet businessman who worked behind the scenes to deliver martial arts instruction to those who couldn't live or train at top academies that produced world-class athletes.

Zenga, along with multiple time jiu-jitsu world champion Bernardo Faria would go on to create what would become BJJSuperdeals and BJJFanatics, two of the leading resources of high-level instruction videos for athletes looking to supplement their local training.

Zenga and Faria have access to the top jiu-jitsu practitioners in the world. Not just any black belts, but world-class/world-champion level black belts. Zenga and Faria reach out and bring these high caliber athletes into the studio to film very focused training videos on various aspects of jiu-jitsu and grappling based martial arts. Then they share these videos as instructional courses. This insight has allowed Zenga to gain special insight into commonalities amongst the very best in sport and in life.

What is one of the leading common denominators of success amongst highly accomplished people? The answer is that they have goals. More specifically, they have well-defined goals. They have big goals, small goals, long-term goals, short-term goals, and goals that lead to additional goals.

The Importance Of Goals

The importance of having goals is nothing new to the breakthroughs in human development. In his highly acclaimed book by author Brian Tracy, "Goals! How To Get Everything You Want – Faster Than You Ever Thought Possible," the New York Times best-selling self-development author explains how goals are used by ambitious people who want to get ahead faster.

Tracy describes the summary statement of all religions, philosophies, metaphysics, psychology, and success as, "You become what you think about the most." Your outer world ultimately becomes a reflection of your inner world. Your outer world of experience mirrors back to you what you think about most of the time.

Tracy gives the example of how living without clear goals is like driving a car in a thick fog. It doesn't matter how well the car is built, or how well the engineering is, you will end up having to drive slowly and hesitantly even on the smoothest of roads. Having goals is like lifting the fog allowing you to focus and channel your energies and abilities toward what you really want. Clear and well-defined goals enable you to step on the gas pedal of your own life and move rapidly towards achieving your personal objectives.

It should be noted that goals are different than dreams or wishes. A goal is something specific, that is clear, written, and measurable. A goal can be quickly and clearly described to another person. A goal is something that is known when you have achieved it or not. It was once said, "Your dreams are only your dreams until you write them down. Then they are goals."

Goals will provide meaning and direction in your life. Happiness and fulfillment come from making forward progress towards your personal goals and objectives even if that progress is hard, challenging, and includes setbacks. Making progress towards goals makes you feel engaged and effective. It energizes you. You build confidence and move towards larger and more challenging goals for improving your abilities along the way. Goals effectively allow you to take charge and command of your own life.

Being clear about what you really want in life is important. Stephen Covey, the author of the runaway bestselling book, "The 7 Habits Of Highly Effective People," stated, "Be sure that, as you scramble up the ladder of success, it is leaning against the right building." You don't want to be one of those people that work their lives away chasing certain items or material goods only to discover at the end of the journey that the joy and satisfaction obtained from the pursuit wasn't worth it. You'll end up asking, "Is this all there is?"

Leaders like Mike Zenga and Travis Stevens accomplish a lot of goals and objectives because they spend a lot of time thinking about their futures. They don't spend a lot of time worrying about the past. Nor do they spend time hung up on the pressures of the present. Their time and energies are spent focusing on what could be changed ahead of them to move them forward. Having a long-term perspective is one of the most important determinants of financial and personal success in life.

This holds true in the world of jiu-jitsu. The journey to black belt and beyond requires years and years of incremental improvements, honing and building skills along the way. Focusing only on the present will keep you too entrenched in the struggles of being perhaps only a white belt, or blue belt, or purple belt. Those are just steps that must be navigated across in the course of your journey. Yet, too many jiu-jitsu practitioners get so wrapped up in the present and the past of getting tapped out or out-positioned that they fail to stay focused on the bigger picture and lose the ability to think several years into the future. As a result, they end up quitting the endeavor.

Alas, they lose out on all the skills and benefits that come along with being a lifetime martial artist. The further you can think into the future and keep perspective on how the present relates to that future, the better decisions you will end up making in the present. This will greatly increase the probabilities that your future goals become a reality.

Peter Drucker, a pioneer in management consulting, corporate education, and author of several important works in the areas of management once stated, "We greatly overestimate what we can accomplish in one year. But we greatly underestimate what we can accomplish in five years." Goals allow you to align your objectives with reasonable time estimates that can keep you moving along the path to success.

Tracy's book, "Goals! How To Get Everything You Want – Faster Than You Ever Thought Possible," is outstanding at laying out and detailing the steps of proper goal setting and the achievement of those goals. Tracy focuses on seven keys to goal setting;

1. Goals must be clear, specific, detailed, and written down. Goals should not be vague or general, like "I want to be happy or make more money."

2. Goals must be measurable and objective. An independent third party should be able to analyze and evaluate those goals. Having a goal like, "I want to make a crapload of money" is more of a dream or wish. Earning a specific amount of money within a reasonable time is a real goal that can be measured, tracked, and benchmarked.

3. Goals must be time bounded. There must be a time schedule, a deadline, or intermediate time standards along the way. There are no goals too big, only time periods too short. Deadlines should be reasonable for the goals you are trying to achieve.

4. Your goals must be challenging. Goals should cause you to stretch outside of your comfort zone. They should move you past the point of anything that you have accomplished in the past. Your goals shouldn't be so low that success is 100% guaranteed because the goal was set too low or too easy to achieve.

5. Your goals must be congruent with your values and in harmony with each other. Your goals should not contradict with one another or go against your own integrity, values, morals, or ethics. Your goals should not work against one another whereby accomplishing one goal would automatically mean failure at another goal.

6. Your goals must be balanced among your career or business, your financial life, your family, your health, your spiritual life, and your community involvement. An out of balance life usually leads to unhappiness and a lack of enjoyment along the journey.

7. You must have a major definite purpose for your life. Accomplishing your overall or main goal in life should help you improve your life more than any other single goal. Have clarity on what that overall goal is and stay focused on what matters along the journey.

Success on the mats, in business, and in life means consistent forward progress towards the higher level of skills. Where those skills end up will be a function of the goals that you set for yourself. One of your biggest responsibilities in life, something that you ultimately will need to hold yourself accountable for, is to manage your time and allocate the appropriate amount of time in pursuit of your goals.

Don't leave your future to chance or randomness. Decide what it is you will stand for. Decide what it is you want to accomplish in life. Decide what is meaningful to you. Take charge of your goals and objectives. Your goals should include career goals, family goals, health goals, financial goals, and personal goals. Some people want to paint pictures or play the piano. Others like to choke out their friends while working up a sweat during personal combat.

Give yourself a chance to succeed in life and on the mats. Countless people come and go through the sport of jiu-jitsu. They come in, train for a bit, and once the novelty wears off and they realize that the path to mastery is a long one, they abandon the path and go back to watching television or surfing the web. Your jiu-jitsu goals should be believable in a way that they are in harmony with your life and with reality.

You may dream about being a world champion. That's not a bad dream to have, but your lifestyle would need to back up that dream. There is far more to jiu-jitsu than just competition medals or chasing world championships. It's estimated that less than 10% of all jiu-jitsu practitioners even compete and only a very tiny sliver of that group can mathematically end up being a champion.

What jiu-jitsu can do for you is the same thing it has done for countless others. It can provide mental stimulation. It's a very technical art that builds on advanced physical and mental problem solving on the fly. Jiu-jitsu can provide a social framework to make friends, build social circles, and have fun with others. There is a lot of laughing with friends while practicing the art. Jiu-jitsu is a wonderful activity to build and maintain your health as you age. There are very few physical activities that require such diverse physical traits as that of jiu-jitsu. Jiu-jitsu will call upon your strength, power, endurance, quickness, agility, mobility, flexibility, and coordination. Those are all wonderful physical characteristics to keep sharp as you age.

Jiu-jitsu will also help in weight management and body composition. It will give you a great source of motivation to eat healthy while maintaining a strong and lean build. Jiu-jitsu will add confidence to other areas of life. That could be from a self-defense standpoint, feeling better about your body, and knowing that you are capable of navigating through physical and mental adversity.

Goals will help you become more successful in business and in life. You don't have to become a world champion to reap the benefits of a jiu-jitsu lifestyle. As Zenga says, "The goals you set and achieve in jiu-jitsu will begin to impact your daily life more and more. Set and focus on your goals."

The lessons of having goals like those of Yuri Simoes, Travis Stevens, or Mike Zenga are clear. You can accomplish far more in life than you ever imagined while having fun and being happy. Not everything will be smooth. There will be obstacles. There will be setbacks. Goals take time to achieve. But it is the very goals that you set for yourself that will allow you to look back on your life with either pride or regret. If you want to have a wonderful jiu-jitsu journey, learn to chase some short-term and medium-term goals while staying on the path to your long-term goals, which should be to become a lifelong martial artist and jiu-jitsu practitioner. Having goals in life will greatly assist you in improving your finances, living healthier, maintaining quality relationships, and finding fulfillment and happiness along the way.

Principle 15: Visualization

"The key to effective visualization is to create the most detailed, clear, and vivid of a mental picture to focus on as possible. The more vivid the visualization, the more likely and quickly you are to begin attracting the things that help you achieve what you want to get done." – Georges St. Pierre, Former UFC Champion

"I can do it. Hit the sequence. Do it just like I practiced over and over again. Stop thinking about the times I messed it up. You can do this..."

All eyes are focused on you as you walk out into the center of that competition arena. It's loudly silent with lurid noises gurgling within your head as if you are underwater. Your brain is scrambling for confidence, reassurance, and working overtime to block out any negative thoughts whatsoever. You've practiced, hours on end, day after day, month after month, year after year. And the injuries, horrible injuries.

But now it's time to test yourself once again and overcome what at times seems like insurmountable fear. Is this even fun? This is human torture. It's insane.

The previous description wasn't the start of a jiu-jitsu match. It was the story of a little girl by the name of Livia Gluchowska, a Polish born gymnast about to turn herself upside down at God awful speeds on a 4-inch-wide block of wood five meters long and elevated 125 centimeters from the floor. That's over four feet, which for a ten-year-old female gymnast is a height that is mentally intimidating since it can be taller than you are at the time.

For all its popularity and glory that comes from watching the Olympics once every four years, competitive gymnastics for young girls comes with a dark side. It means terrible injuries. It means fear. It means body composition issues and eating disorders that come from a power-to-weight game that is applied to children. It means no normal social life playing with your friends. It's all consuming. It's everything. It is every day in the gym and every weekend at competitions. This is the life of competitive juvenile gymnastics.

Competitive gymnastics is a sport that breeds pressure. It's about winning, which only comes from perfection. There is no room for anything less than perfect. Winning does not bring everlasting joy but rather only temporary relief that you didn't fail like everybody else while striving for gold. Winning on the weekend is just a reprieve from the reality that when you get back to the gym on Monday morning, it will be your mandate to take the skills and risks up a notch, elevate your tricks, improve your art, and develop your amazing abilities by working on even more difficult tasks. Attempting more difficult tasks will inevitably result in more injuries, more pressure, and more fear. It's a vicious circle. It's the constant and never-ending quest to do seemingly impossible human gravity defying flips and feats.

Fast forward two decades and Livia Gluchowska is now immersed in a new personal passion called jiu-jitsu. She's no longer living in Poland and is out of Europe after moving to Australia. She's years removed from her competitive gymnastics career which ended at the washed up geriatric old age of nineteen.

But now armed with that experience and knowledge that came with being a competitive gymnast during her childhood is reaping the rewards as an adult. She no longer must do flips to perfection with the risk of breaking her neck or snapping a leg in front of countless eyes. She only needs to choke another human being out for her own satisfaction.

Gluchowska is a student (and now black belt) under the tutelage of Lachlan Giles, the head coach and high-level competitor in Melbourne, Australia. Melbourne is the hotspot for jiu-jitsu in Australia, and it's common to see the Australian superstars like Craig Jones or Kit Dale on the mats.

Gluchowska is a multiple time world champion. She has won jiu-jitsu competition gold medals as a blue, purple, and brown belt and has recently been promoted to black belt. She has been successful in the gi and no-gi competitions, winning titles in IBJJF events while also competing at the highest levels in no-Gi such as the ADCC trials.

What sets a competitor like Gluchowska apart from the others? It's multiple items. She has honed the craft of being a disciplined and hardworking committed athlete since she was just a tiny child. She's grown accustomed to pain, injuries, and obstacles that come along in elite level sports. But beyond the physical, Gluchowska is mentally strong in ways that few humans are.

When you live in Melbourne, Australia but your competition is on the other side of the earth at a World Championship event in the United States, you must step off that airplane, get to the event center and win immediately. In jiu-jitsu competitions, it's win or go-home. There are no second attempts. You are missing work, your family and friends, and your training, to spend an awful lot of money to travel to a competition that will last only a few minutes in duration. That's just the reality of the game.

If an athlete cannot focus when it matters, then it's not going to turn out well. The competition is too stiff. The athletes at that level are too good. Everybody is well trained and in top shape. But Gluchowska can visualize her success well before the competition has even begun. Gluchowska is a winner, and winners visualize the rewards of success rather than the penalties of failure.

Visualization As A Life Tool

Visualization is a technique that has been around for a long-time but is now being adapted and used by the world's most successful people. Visualization is seeing the goal as already complete in your mind's eye. Visualization allows one to dream up possibilities along with envisioning all the steps and processes that must be mastered to make the dream a reality.

Oprah Winfrey has said, "Create the highest, grandest vision possible for your life, because you become what you believe." Wayne Dyer, the well-known but now deceased self-help author, motivational speaker, and philosopher has stated, "In order to make a visualization a reality in the world of form, you must be willing to do whatever it takes to make it happen."

We are all chasing fulfillment. We all have dreams. We all aspire to do greater things. Visualization is the combination of envisioning the life that brings you true fulfillment while breaking down all the steps necessary to make those dreams an actual reality. Visualization done right can change physiology. Athletes imagining themselves in competition will elevate their heart rates, their palms can get sweaty, they will feel the nerves of the competition as if they are in the competition. Visualization is mentally rehearsing what must be done successfully to accomplish your goals. It is extremely powerful.

Mental training has been called the science of success. It can be applied to jiu-jitsu, but more importantly, it can be applied to many areas of life and various life scenarios. You stand to benefit tremendously from the knowledge and techniques that lie at the root of visualization. Mental training and visualization can help take you to all new levels of performance, achievement, and personal success.

In his best-selling book, "The Art of Mental Training – A Guide To Performance Excellence" author DC Gonzalez shares his experience and knowledge that was based on working under P.C. Siegel, a world-renowned sports and peak performance authority, sports hypnotherapist, and Neuro Linguistics

Programming (NLP) Master Practitioner. Gonzalez shares the insights that he acquired while working his own multi-decade client list that included top athletes, executives, actors, pro-fighters, musicians, military soldiers, and other professionals. What Gonzales makes clear is that, "Whatever is going on inside your head has everything to do with how well you end up performing." The science is backing up the insights and experience of Gonzales.

In addition to being a peak performance coach and the author of the book "The Art of Mental Training," which is relevant to experts in all different areas of expertise and fields of study, the author is also a black belt in jiu-jitsu. Visualization doesn't just apply to jiu-jitsu. It applies to many endeavors of life on and off the mats.

A Champion Visualizes Success

Mackenzie Dern is a multiple time IBJJF World Champion in both Gi and no-Gi competitions along with championships in Abu Dhabi World Pro, Pans, and IBJJF European Championships. She has won many of those championships in both her weight class of 129.0 pounds and the absolute division where she had to face much bigger and stronger opponents. Dern, for all intents and purposes, was born and raised on the martial arts mats. The daughter of top black belt practitioner Wellington "Megaton" Dias, Dern competed in judo and jiu-jitsu tournaments since she was just a toddler. She developed fast and joined the adult division at the tender young age of 14.

Competing against adults when you are barely a teenager could be a daunting task. The pressure of pleasing your parents, the fear of losing, the over-whelming nerves of combat sports and the long waits at event centers can crack the attitudes of the best of them. But Dern has a knack for controlling her internal mental climate. She can visualize her success long before it becomes a reality. Dern has learned that the right attitude helps empower her to take the necessary actions and to focus on the things that must be done. It's the positive attitude and commitment to winning that makes all the difference.

A good attitude allows one to visualize success. The vision of success creates optimism and positive energy, and it is that same positive energy that is necessary to set good things in motion. Negative energy is limiting and restrictive. A negative attitude will create visions of failure and will always work against you.

Successful people teach themselves the skill of changing their own mental thoughts. Negative results are just temporary setbacks that are used as learning tools along the way. Negative results are opportunities in disguise. They allow oneself to see where they need improvement, what needs to be changed, or where to put more focus and energy on to finally break through with higher-level performances and abilities. It's about reaching one's potential.

Author Gonzales emphasizes this point, "A bad attitude can cost a person everything. It affects not only how you feel, but also how you perform." If you can't visualize a positive outcome and overcoming the hurdles and obstacles that are surely going to come your way, you are doomed from the start.

Every successful person and champion knows that the key to climbing to the heights of success is based upon stepping up and over all the obstacles that develop along the way.

Champions can close their eyes and watch a movie in their own mind of themselves in pursuit of their goals. They allow these movies to bring them back to past victories when they were strong and unstoppable. They could vividly recall the thrill of the game and the joy that they experienced allowing themselves to relive those memories repeatedly at will when they need to prepare for a challenging task. These visualizations allow them to have the positive attitude and confidence to then go and do the necessary work and tasks required to accomplish their goals.

The visualizations are so clear that they allow the person to feel the physical sensations of being there in the present moment. They can hear the crowd. They can feel their heart rate pulsing. They can see their competition moving around and them reacting to the scenarios playing out in their head. These visualizations are all positive mental images with strong feelings attached to them that are wrapped in joy and triumph. They can see themselves victorious and can imagine doing the tasks required to be victorious. What starts in the mind bleeds to the body.

Successful jiu-jitsu practitioners have an ability to stay mentally focused not just during competition but during their daily lives. They know their long-term goals and comprehend that obstacles and roadblocks are part of the journey. By staying focused mentally, they can interrupt negative self-talk and images the moment they start to pop up in their minds. From there, they can change the images from negative to positive.

Successful people in all occupations can imagine success. Successful people visualize the positive outcomes long before they happen. Visualization allows them to concentrate on showing their own brains exactly what it is they want to achieve. Knowing this ahead of time, they can put forth the strategies and training that will be required to achieve those goals and they can pursue those objectives with confidence and realistic expectations during the hard training.

Performing at the highest levels which allow you to work to your human potential is a paradoxical state. It requires you to be amped up, focused, and with a heightened state of awareness. But underneath the adrenaline rush, nerves, and over-stimulation of the situation, you must find relaxation. Relaxation is important because when used with visualization it facilitates and allows your inner subconscious mind to clearly see your success imagery and feel your success throughout your body.

The ability to calm the mind and relax the body through breathing and meditation while under duress is something that can be practiced and trained. It takes awareness, and one must learn why this is important and more importantly how to do it. Doing it at higher and higher levels and with better results comes from experience and repetition. Your first time giving a speech, running a meeting, teaching a class, performing at an elite gymnastics competition, or participating in a jiu-jitsu tournament won't be your smoothest run.

That's what gives elite performers the edge against others in their field. They have more experience being on the big stage and knowing the requirements to elevate their performance when the stakes are most high.

When you look at successful practitioners on the jiu-jitsu mats like Livia Gluchowska or Mackenzie Dern, you can see the results of using the critical elements of mental success as described by DC Gonzalez in the book, "The Art of Mental Training." These top performers use positive self-talk like other champions. They properly prepare themselves mentally to battle against top rivals and competitors. They can get in the right state of mind before their event through breathing and visualization.

Principle 16: Ego

"If your ego starts out, 'I am important, I am big, I am special,' you're in for some disappointments when you look around at what we've discovered about the universe. No, you're not big. No, you're not. You're small in time and in space. And you have this frail vessel called the human body that's limited on Earth." – Neil deGrasse Tyson

Jiu-Jitsu has an enormously high rate of turnover and quitting with practitioners. New excited white belts walk into academies with all the dreams of being a dominant grappler only to discover that the path to success in jiu-jitsu is paved with the stones of uncountable failures.

The first few months of jiu-jitsu is an exercise in frustration and failure, often at the hands of smaller and physically weaker opponents who may not look that tough when the fist bump occurs at the start of the roll. Soon you find yourself wrapped up like a pretzel with not enough blood flowing to the brain. Or, one of your joints is about to be flexed in the opposite direction than it was made to move.

Day after day you will fumble through techniques that look so easy from the instructor doing the demonstration. Day after day you will have to tap out. Sometimes, due to your own inexperience, you will tap out a bit too late which results in a tweaked muscle, a strain of a ligament, a pop of a joint, or you will get choked out. These are hard and humbling lessons and realities.

Yet again, jiu-jitsu is an analogy to life. Life is full of failure for all who strive to exceed themselves. Life is full of setbacks, obstacles, losing, getting knocked down but getting back up. Yet, like life, most people quit well before they achieve any level of success. Their own ego gets in the way of the very thing that they desire which is more success. It's another one of those paradoxical attributes of living life as a human. Failure is just something that successful people have capitalized on more than the typical person. Successful individuals learn to master their own ego, move on, learn from those failures, and never let those failures stop them from reaching their potential and their goals.

Ego Can Be Dangerous

Jocko Willink, the former Navy Seal, top podcaster, and black-belt jiu-jitsu practitioner talks a lot about ego and humility. He understands that ego and humility is more than just a small differentiator between individuals. Ego and humility may not just be the difference between success and failure on a task, but in certain circumstances, may mean the difference between life and death itself.

While training Navy Seals and commanding elite task teams, Willink was often responsible for firing soldiers from leadership positions. The reason wasn't a lack of competency or courage, but rather a lack of humility. As Willink describes, "When you lack humility, you can't listen to anybody else."

Willink continues, "Not only that, when you lack humility, you don't respect your enemy or your competitor. And when you don't respect your enemy, you stop training hard. Now is when you start cutting corners. And when you take shortcuts and stop training, that is when you get caught and killed. The worst thing about a lack of humility is that if you lack humility, you can't even do a solid and honest assessment of yourself. It usually means that you're not going to improve."

A Champion Controls Their Ego

It was 2009 at the ADCC championships. One of the most significant and prestigious submission grappling tournaments in the world. In a semi-final match in the 88kg division, it was a battle of world champions. Carlos Machado black belt Rafael Lovato Jr. was set to face off against Braulio Estima.

Braulio Estima and his brother Victor were two brothers that were at the highest level of jiu-jitsu competitors. The advantage that high-level jiu-jitsu siblings have is that they possess built in training partners with each other no different than other famous jiu-jitsu siblings such as the Mendes Brothers (Guilherme and Rafael), the Miyao Brothers (Paulo and João) and the Ribeiro Brothers (Saulo and Xande). This allowed for unending drilling and practicing between family members. It was Gracie jiu-jitsu basics at their finest. A family that fights together stays together.

During training leading up to the ADCC competition, Victor was struggling with Braulio's inverted guard. Braulio would twist, turn, and spin while keeping his feet connected to Victor's hips and his upper legs at all times. This becomes very frustrating for anyone going against an opponent with a good inverted game. But during a practice roll, Victor managed to trap one of Braulio's feet between his arm and his abdomen. A lightbulb went off for both, and they began working on details to convert this position into a new technique.

By the time the ADCC tournament came around, Braulio had the finishing details refined to the point where he could perform them at the highest level of competition. During his semi-final match with Rafael Lovato Jr., he applied the foot lock which traps the foot of the bottom guard player in the abdomen of the standing player, figure-fouring the ankle while throwing the hips forward. It creates a mix of a heel hook and toe hold and quickly becomes dangerous. Lovato would tap out to what later and justifiably would become known as "The Estima Lock."

Two years later in 2011, it would be the younger Estima, Victor who would finish every single one of his opponents by submission in the World No-Gi Championships with the Estima Lock. It was then that people really started to take notice of this new technique and devastating threat.

Beyond the foot lock that bears his name, what Braulio Estima has learned from jiu-jitsu and applied to his greater life is his tremendous lack of ego and humility as a human. "I don't believe just because you are a champion or the best in the world at something, you are a better or more important person than somebody else. I treat a white belt no different than a black belt off of the mats. We are all equal as people. I just happen to do my job well and put a lot of effort into jiu-jitsu. It doesn't mean I am better than somebody else in life," says Estima.

From Student To Master Instructor

Caio Terra, a 12-time world champion has a fast-growing academy affiliate program. He is working very hard to build this affiliate program to spread the word of jiu-jitsu beyond the martial art itself. Humble and authentically caring, Terra knows how hard life can be and how we all struggle to make it through life itself. Jiu-jitsu gives us the tools to navigate life in a more efficient capacity. The path to those efficiencies is through better techniques of dealing with obstacles, no different than rolling on the mats. But to build the technique, one must let go of the ego in training. If all someone thinks about is over-powering their training partner, winning, and getting the tap, they sacrifice working on technique. Eventually, age will set in, power and strength will subside, and the person will be void of technique which could have been used for the rest of their lives.

Terra describes his ambitions to spread his message, "People that teach jiu-jitsu should be good people. You shouldn't look for the best competitor. You should look for somebody who has a good heart that will not just teach you jiu-jitsu but will help you with life."

Jiu-jitsu, as in life, requires a tremendous amount of balancing abilities. Not so much the physical requirements of balance, although that is a tremendous asset in the sport of jiu-jitsu, but balancing our time, priorities, and most importantly our inner persona. A successful person must have ambitions. They must have skills. They must have drive and work ethic. They must strive to achieve great things. Along the way to chasing their potential, they may experience many victories and receive many acknowledgements and recognition.

As victories and recognitions accumulate, along with the core skills and abilities, so often does the inner ego. Psychologists are aware that a super strong ego can result with someone overly focused on themselves and with disregard for anyone and everybody else. Ego can and often does lead to an unhealthy belief in our own importance. Ego begins to equate with arrogance as the person moves from trying to better themselves to bettering others while demanding to be recognized as being better than everybody else. Thus, balancing confidence and superiority can be a tricky game.

Success in jiu-jitsu and success in life can lead us to develop a large ego rather than help us control our own ego to foster future learning and personal development. At certain points in your jiu-jitsu journey, you may not want to compete or train with certain people because of a fear of getting beat. This is the wrong mindset because the goal is to improve your skills and become a better person rather than salvage or maintain your ego.

You will find yourself in these paradoxes. You may try and emphasize humility, but that will require at times keeping your self-image in check. Jiu-jitsu is about training through failure and learning the lessons from the failure. It's not about maximizing your own ego.

Using Ego To Get Better As A Person

Tom DeBlass was exhausted. He drove two hours in traffic from his home in New Jersey to take a class from John Danaher at the famed Renzo Gracie Academy in New York City. DeBlass is an important influencer to many in the jiu-jitsu community. He's a positive role model. A black belt under grappling sensation and former UFC standout Ricardo Almeida, DeBlass is no stranger to the competitive podiums. He's won world championships, Pan American Championships, and matches in the ADCC. He's competed at the highest level of the sport. DeBlass was a fast learner who didn't even start his jiu-jitsu career until the age of 19. He was a black belt 6 ½ years later and has his own jiu-jitsu school in Orange County, New Jersey.

But on this morning, it would be DeBlass that would force himself to be the student. Always learning, always drilling, always pushing himself. He's not afraid to transition from the teacher back to a student and practice with some of the toughest guys in the sport who often are dedicated to training 100% of the time rather than running businesses like himself. After the class, the drilling sessions began followed by live sparring. He trained as hard as he could to the point of exhaustion. He's been known to train so hard that blue belts will begin to dominate him. But he leaves his ego at home. He's not afraid to look bad in the training room if it means he looks better in competition.

The idea of training is to get moving, get sweaty, get exhausted and work on technique. As DeBlass explains, "It's easy to sit and wait until everyone is tired and then jump in and train. But you have to ask yourself, do you want to be a training room champion or a real champion?"

In our current society filled with social media, glamour, and instant gratification, ego will be a difficult challenge to control. Our culture relishes success, victory, and self-importance. We can brag to anyone and everyone willing to listen on the internet. We are supposed to live big, think big, and act big. We are all supposed to achieve huge success in life.

These expectations in and of themselves can create tremendous conflict with us as we pursue personal development and self-improvement. Yes, we should seek to improve. Yes, we should pursue personal success. Yes, ego is essential to anyone that really wants to be exceptional. Ego is, and always will be a circular exercise.

Ryan Holiday is a best-selling author with books such as, "The Obstacle Is The Way" which made the Wall Street Journal and USA Today bestseller lists. Holiday wrote the book on Ego entitled, "Ego Is The Enemy." Holiday's claim is that although many history books are filled with tales of obsessive visionary geniuses who remade the world in their image with sheer, almost irrational force, history is also made by individuals who fought their egos at every turn, who eschewed the spotlight, and who put their higher goals above their desire for personal recognition.

Holiday explains the cycle of ego in an easy to understand fashion, "At any given time in life, people find themselves at one of three stages.   1. We're aspiring to something – trying to make a dent in the universe. 2. We have achieved success – perhaps a little, perhaps a lot, or 3. We have failed – recently or continually. Most of us are in these stages in a fluid sense – we're aspiring until we succeed, we succeed until we fail or until we aspire to more, and after we fail we can begin to aspire or succeed again."

In a sense, Holiday gets his readers to understand that ego can be a cycle of three stages; aspire, success, and failure and that managing one's ego through these stages is essential for harnessing the positive aspects of ego. This approach leads to personal success yet at the same time allows you to manage the negative aspects of ego that can lead to crushing personal failures.

Managing your ego is about analyzing your weaknesses objectively so that you can learn to deal with those weaknesses. Your desire to be "right" is usually stronger and more powerful than your need to find out what is true. This human behavioral flaw is what often gets us into trouble. We like believing our own opinions without properly stress testing them. We don't like to reflect on our mistakes and weaknesses. We usually don't like honest feedback from others if it isn't "positive praise." All these factors lead to blind spots within us even though we believe that we see everything correctly. Ego thus requires us to replace the need for being "right" with the need for figuring out what is true.

You may be an aspiring jiu-jitsu practitioner or business person such as Jocko Willink, Braulio Estima, or Tom DeBlass or you may be looking to apply your efforts or talents in other endeavors even outside of jiu-jitsu. During your journey you will have to learn how to harness the power of ego such that you remain grounded, hardened, and focused, rather than delusional, self-absorbed, and self-destructing. How is one to be great, yet humble? You could learn a lot through the examples of plenty of jiu-jitsu leaders such as Caio Terra, Braulio Estima, or Tom DeBlass who are as much leaders off the mats as they are on the mats.

Ego is an asset and a personal demon that must be managed, trained, and contained each day. It is like training itself. Italian author, university professor, and martial artist Daniele Bolelli is the philosophical writer who wrote the book, "On The Warrior's Path." Daily practice is essential for success. As he states, "Training is like sweeping the floor. Just because we've done it once, doesn't mean the floor is clean forever. Every day the dust comes back. Every day we must sweep."

Principle 17: Habit

"We are what we repeatedly do. Success is not an action but a habit." – Aristotle

Jokes don't write themselves. Nor is the first draft of a joke the eventual keeper that makes it into the final act at the big performance special. Comedians are secretly obsessive workaholics who focus on their craft, spinning their words in just the right order, cadence, and verbiage to deliver a piercing sensation into the brain of the audience to generate a laugh response. It's not just the words, it's the timing and delivery. It's your physical mannerisms. It's your fascial expressions. It's acting on a stage.

Every week, he writes jokes. Every week, he researches. Every week, he exercises. Every week, he eats well. Every week, the schedule is so packed that there isn't a lot of time wasted on sitting around doing nothing. He's always busy and doing something.

Joe Rogan is a comedian, television host, hugely successful podcaster, health enthusiast, UFC commentator, and a jiu-jitsu black belt. He's a master of personal habits. Rogan's additional talent is attracting all kinds of haters on social media who seem to miss all the value from his shared personal gems on what really is at the core of his success. He's an incredibly sharing individual that practices what he preaches and doesn't hold back.

What most people focus on are the accomplishments of Rogan. That's our society. We live in a culture that equates success with a tangible positive result; a championship ring, a million dollars, a mansion, or six-pack abs. That's how most determine their heroes, glorify them, and define their success to others. However, focusing on the end result, and not the mundane things that were behind achieving the success is the biggest mistake people make when trying to improve their own personal lives.

Are you congratulating yourself for the IBJJF medal, the belt promotion, the 10 pounds lost, or are you congratulating yourself for doing the daily actions that were required to achieve the end result? If you can't do the daily actions consistently, there will be no consistent positive end results. One only comes after the other.

Rogan has learned how to gain satisfaction and fulfillment by accomplishing the small steps and making gradual improvements that were required for him to reach many of his goals. If he didn't learn how to reward himself for the small steps of constantly writing jokes, even if they didn't make the cut, then he would never accumulate enough winning jokes that make up an entire performance.

The same holds true in jiu-jitsu. You may want to achieve a black belt or any advanced colored belt, but the belt promotion is the end result of doing a lot of daily actions over a sustained period of time. Those daily actions are your personal habits, the essential ingredient to your potential. Can you get on the mats, practice your techniques, keep a healthy diet, get plenty of sleep for recovery, and learn the small details that add up to big breakthroughs in your jiu-jitsu game?

People identify with Rogan as a successful leader, a podcaster, a TV star, a martial artist, and a comedian. But what preceded others from identifying Rogan as all those things was Rogan identifying himself as all those things. He had to create the habits necessary to become proficient in all those activities. Nobody is born with all the information and habits to become successful in something, let alone many things. Habits are something that are acquired and developed through self-reflection and commitment to your preferred identity and self-image.

Rogan had to first believe that he was a comedian, a TV host, a jiu-jitsu practitioner, a podcaster, and that he could at least dedicate the necessary time and effort to learn how to become those things. He had to create an internal identity and self-image of who he wanted to become and more importantly, who he did not want to become.

The first step in changing habits is believing that you can change as a person. It's the internal belief that none of us are fixed permanently as humans and that growth is possible. Your self-image of yourself becomes a crucial component of change. Without a clear idea of your preferred self-image, it will be difficult to be congruent between your identity or self-image and the newly desired habits that will be required for that future identity and self-image. Further, positive behaviors and habits will lead to continued changes in self-image and identity as you gain confidence in your ability to be who it is you are striving to become through the hard work of personal growth.

Creating a new self-image and personal identity requires changing the underlying habits that will move you from being your "old-self" to your "new-self." It's the daily habits that make the difference in the metamorphosis. You can see this in people that lose massive amounts of weight. Through that weight loss, they obtain large amounts of personal confidence and become more socially and physically active. You can also see it in people that go through an educational process like a college degree. They often come out the other side of the process as a credentialed professional and they possess a more confident and future outlook for themselves.

Many times, you won't have any real idea how far you can go or what you will become because you are still transitioning from your old identity and self-image to your new identity and self-image. There often is no way of knowing what your human potential is in most fields of study because you are denied the opportunity to try everything that interests you to the fullest extent which would require years of hard work and then rewind the years and only focus on the things that led to the best outcomes. You will have to choose your goals beforehand without knowing how it will turn out. Following your heart then is a gamble in many ways.

Changing Your Future By Acquiring New Habits

Imagine being born in an ordinary run-of-the-mill little town with a population of fewer than 7,000 residents like

Cobleskill, New York. You do what you thought you should do. You go to school, play some baseball, and then go off to college dreaming of becoming a major league baseball player. You select a college in Tampa, Florida where the weather is far more conducive to baseball than the cold weather of Cobleskill, New York to chase your dream. But then the reality sets in. At only 6 feet tall and 180 pounds, you lack the physical size and skills to make a pro career out of baseball. You are only another statistic in the pyramid of college and major league sports.

You go off to the real world and do something predictable and sane, like obtain a job at an insurance company to become a corporate professional and make enough money to start a life as a practical adult. Along the way you stumble upon jiu-jitsu and martial arts to help make sense of life, give you an outlet, and get in some workouts while getting some enjoyment out of exercise. As time progresses, you are still going into the office every day and begin wondering, "Is this it? Is this what my life is going to be like for another 40 years?"

You must make a choice. Do you keep your professional job in the insurance industry and take the safe and well-paved path of life or do you hit the eject button and escape through the emergency exit? As previously mentioned, you don't get to live multiple lives and then go back and select the one that turned out the best. You must make choices and live with the results of those choices.

This was the exact scenario for Matt Arroyo. Arroyo would relocate from Cobleskill, New York to Tampa to pursue baseball at the University of Tampa. As luck would have it, Arroyo would stumble into a jiu-jitsu and fight academy under the leadership of Rob Kahn. Kahn just happened to be one of

Royce Gracie's first students and would become Royce's first black belt in the United States.

Arroyo would begin mixed martial arts training under the tutelage of Kahn, and soon enough was asking to fight inside the cage in mixed martial arts competitions. That's a completely different identity and self-image of an insurance salesperson working at a corporate desk. The daily habits of a mixed martial arts fighter are quite different than those of a professional insurance salesperson. Arroyo had to make a choice. Was he to spend his time building habits and putting in the necessary work to become an insurance professional or would he build a new dream of becoming a cage fighter and jiu-jitsu practitioner?

Arroyo would make a choice that very few people would make in real life. He chose to quit his professional job and dedicate his life to martial arts without any idea how things would turn out.

Fortunately, Kahn's jiu-jitsu instruction was systematized in a way that was very "Gracie-like" which was focused on fighting and self-defense. It wasn't for point fighting or earning advantages in IBJJF competitions. It was about controlling your opponent to end the fight either through submission or strikes. This was exactly what the evolving fighter Arroyo would need in his early progression and transition into martial arts and real-life fighting.

In his first cage fight in September of 2006 in a small arena in Orlando, Florida, Arroyo would win his fight in 0:56 seconds via rear-naked choke. A fighter was officially born. Less than 7 weeks later, he would lose a fight in Tampa in a promotion called, "Real Fighting Championships 7: Night of Champions" against an unheralded and unknown fighter by the name of

Matt Brown. No matter how many times or how hard Arroyo hit Brown or how many times he moved in for positions that would put himself in line for a submission, Brown would find a way to endure and move forward.

Brown would win that fight by a technical knockout and would go on to become a major star and fan favorite in the UFC by the nickname "The Immortal." Arroyo went back to the drawing board and would fight for the same promotion in Tampa again the following February defeating his opponent in the first round via triangle choke. Through Kahn, Royce Gracie, and the connections to the UFC, Arroyo applied and was selected to be on the UFC reality show "The Ultimate Fighter: Team Hughes vs. Team Serra" fighting on Team Serra.

The former insurance sales professional would go on to win fights in the UFC, be on the undercard of UFC 94: Georges St. Pierre vs. BJ Penn 2, and be featured in the video game UFC Undisputed 2009. What led to this remarkable change in life direction? What changed were all new fundamental habits that put Arroyo in a position to succeed at new life goals. He created a new self-image and then instilled the habits to transform himself into that self-image.

If you want to upgrade your life, you need to upgrade your habits and figure out which habits are needed to be developed and implemented in your life at this very moment. Old habits and bad habits need to be replaced with new habits and good habits. A person who works a corporate job, comes home, and eats fast food and watches TV for hours each night has completely different habits than a martial artist that is seeking to find out what his or her human potential is.

Habits influence the follow up habits. Momentum is built as consistency is implemented. When a new habit like physical training for competition is implemented, it is common for people to naturally want to start eating better (a whole new set of habits). Habits are built upon former habits, and those habits will impact all areas of your life from exercise, nutrition, communication, mental awareness, sleep, time management, who you associate with, and being responsible for your own actions.

Hacking Into New Habits

Derek Doepker, author of the book, "The Healthy Habit Revolution – Create Better Habits In 5 Minutes A Day" describes how important your identity is and how there are even ways to "hack" the habit-forming system to more quickly develop and build positive habits. The first step to creating habits is transforming your self-image or identity to believe that you can become something better as a person. But what happens when you have a hard time believing that identity early in the game? What if you really don't believe in yourself when trying to make changes as a person?

Doepker describes how habits eventually change the way you identify with yourself. You may hear people describe themselves such as, "I am a jiu-jitsu practitioner" or "I am a guitar player." They use the words, "my" or "I am" when describing themselves or what they do. Using the words first, before the activity or action is what is called an "affirmation."

Words are powerful to the brain. If you are having a hard time believing you can change, simply stating the words to yourself can impact your brain and your internal belief system. That means that changing your language can, potentially over time, change your beliefs and identity. Using affirmations that are believable are effective for reinforcing a new identity. This causes the brain to start to change what it focuses on that is needed for the very changes you wish to make.

Whether you are Joe Rogan or Matt Arroyo, you must believe that you can become a new version of yourself. That new version of yourself will only be created if you form the habits necessary to become that new person. Without the new habits, you will simply revert to your old self soon enough and never make the necessary changes for long-term self-improvement.

You will never know what your potential is or what you can or will become in life with certainty. That's just not how life works. There are no guarantees as far as outcome. What is more of a guarantee is that by changing your underlying habits, you will change as a person. As you change as a person, you will be able to change your identity and self-image of yourself and grow into a better version of yourself. How you spend your time and resources are important decisions that you must make for yourself.

Success in jiu-jitsu and in life will require a multitude of personal habits that support the ambitions you have for yourself. Investing the time and energy into building positive habits is well worth the efforts. Without good habits, you are almost assured to never reach your potential.

Principle 18: Become An Artist

"Art enables us to find ourselves and lose ourselves at the same time." – Thomas Merton

There is a saying that if someone is really living a life of art, then they are always smiling. How could so much hard work, obstacles, and human suffering bring so many smiles as it does in jiu-jitsu? It's because jiu-jitsu is an art. It's a martial "art." It's a lifestyle. Pablo Picasso said it best when he stated, "The purpose of art is washing the dust of daily life off our souls."

When someone starts doing jiu-jitsu, they aren't starting the endeavor because they believe it is a path to riches, or financial security, or a better job. They start jiu-jitsu because deep down they have a suspicion that practicing the art will lead to a better life. A richer life. A fuller life. A life of discipline. A life of friendships. A life of meaning. A life of bliss. A life of better health both physically and mentally.

There are many outlets in the pursuit of personal art in life. Some may want to paint a canvas. Some may want to write a song. Some may want to take a photograph. Jiu-jitsu practitioners want to practice a physical art that flows like water through the rocks in the stream of life.

As the level of art progresses, confidence is gained. It helps in so many ways as you navigate life. Art makes you think about life as something other than grinding out a 9-to-5 job that you hate. Art has an interesting way of getting you to travel outside your normal geographic routine of work, the grocery store, and your favorite place to eat.

Art is the thing that you enjoy doing when you are living your life. It's the motivation to get out of bed beyond the search for resources like money or food. Art is beyond money. Art is what changes your life by inspiring you to create. When you create art, you create confidence which transcends into other areas of your life. Art gives you more self-esteem and translates cultures. It inspires others to create art of their own and appreciate the inputs and efforts of others who are willing to share their arts.

Living An Artistic Life On And Off The Mats

When Stuart Cooper began his jiu-jitsu career, he certainly was not a standout. He was quiet, timid, and introverted. His athletic abilities were nothing noteworthy. But he took his licks as a white belt just like everybody else and slowly started figuring out the foreign language of jiu-jitsu. By blue belt, Cooper was secretly convinced that he wanted jiu-jitsu to be a big part of his life and livelihood. To him, it was worth dedicating himself fully to the endeavor as it would somehow lead to greater opportunities. He knew that a 9-to-5 job working for some big company was nothing like the life he could bear for the rest of his career, no matter the salary and financial benefits.

Cooper had a run of bad luck that ultimately led to his calling and opportunities in jiu-jitsu. He would break his arm which resulted in a 12-month break from jiu-jitsu training. Soon after returning to the mats, he broke his foot which prevented him from physically training with all the other participants in the class. Cooper still loved jiu-jitsu and wanted to be on the mats and close to jiu-jitsu. He thought if he bought a video camera, he could film the classes, tournaments, and document the guys on the team. It started out as a fun way to pass the time while still being connected to the jiu-jitsu mats.

Cooper started uploading some of his videos to YouTube and the internet. Soon he would be getting a lot of positive feedback and comments on his videos which encouraged him to move it forward and continue in his new-found personal art which mixed video equipment, the sport of jiu-jitsu, and the underlying stories of the athletes.

He would film a seminar given by Ryan Hall which he created into a seminar instructional and uploaded it online. It was an immediate hit generating thousands of views and comments in a single day. At that moment, Cooper figured out he was onto something unique where he could bring his own insights, style, art, and creative talents to mini-film making.

Soon "Stuart Cooper Films" were viewed and loved by thousands of jiu-jitsu enthusiasts around the world as Cooper would create mini-documentaries of some of the top athletes and characters in the sport of jiu-jitsu. He would focus on the lifestyle of full-time jiu-jitsu practitioners who often lived on the mats and sacrifice for years at a time. These practitioners did not do the art for the money but rather for the love of the art of jiu-jitsu.

Cooper's films share a common thread, that jiu-jitsu can and does change the lives of those who practice the art. Whether it is building confidence, bonding with friends, getting in shape, chasing competition, or learning how to better navigate life's obstacles, Cooper's films provide a ray of peaceful light for those who can relate to the seductive lifestyle of practitioners. Life is hard, jiu-jitsu is very hard, but somehow by practicing jiu-jitsu, life gets easier and better.

What we see through the characters in jiu-jitsu is art within art. It's levels of art that stretch wide and deep. The art of various unique practitioners is expressed on the mats and off the mats. Creativity is all around us with new techniques, new terminology, new training methods, new strategies, new fashion and training gear, and all kinds of ways to express yourself with individuality that can be shared with others.

Podcasters are artists, as are photographers, as are instructors, as are competitors. It's all art within a bigger blanket of art that is never-ending. Cooper, now a black belt and an instructor himself in jiu-jitsu is just an example of what kinds of opportunities exist in jiu-jitsu and life when you submerse yourself into something greater than yourself.

The art can come in a variety of styles and formats. It's building and having the confidence to share your unique insights and talents with others. Cooper found his through his insights behind a camera and his ability to edit stories. That's not the only way for a person to share and contribute to the art of jiu-jitsu or life off the mats.

"Creativity is allowing yourself to make mistakes. Art is knowing which ones to keep." – Scott Adams

Sometimes the world just needs a good shake up when nobody is expecting it. The world of jiu-jitsu got a good shake up when it wasn't expecting it in 2003 that forever changed the trajectory of jiu-jitsu with a very artful twist.

Edgar Cano was a rather unlikely person to make an impact on tens of thousands of grapplers around the world when he was born. Born in Santa Ana, California with Mexican heritage, he would have an upbringing with step-parents. His biological father was from Chihuahua, Mexico and his mother from Guadalajara, Mexico. As luck and geography would have it, Southern California was a new-found home for Mexicans looking for a better way of life and also a growing hub of jiu-jitsu with the Gracie's leading the way in the Los Angeles area.

Cano would later legally change his name to that of his stepfather, and soon enough Edgar Cano would be much more known for the name that now identifies him as Eddie Bravo. Bravo enjoyed grappling as early as high-school and became a member of his high school wrestling team. But his passion was music, and after high-school, the motivated and determined Bravo set off to Hollywood to pursue a music career.

Upon arriving in Hollywood, Bravo would begin taking karate lessons in the early 1990's. By the mid 1990's the UFC entered the picture where the Gracie's introduced jiu-jitsu to the world that demonstrated the effectiveness of the martial art especially for those with smaller physical attributes. Bravo was intrigued enough by what he saw on those early UFC matches to begin training jiu-jitsu under the instruction of Jean Jacques Machado while practicing other martial arts such as Jeet Kune Do.

By 1998 Bravo would be dedicating himself to jiu-jitsu as his only martial art. It wasn't long before Bravo would be bringing his own flare and unique approach to the art with signature moves and sequences such as his "rubber guard," "twister," and "half-guard lockdown."

In 2003, Bravo's artistic approach to modernizing an already modern martial art would cement his legacy and put him on a path all to his own. Bravo won the 145lbs/66kg North American ADCC trials as a brown belt and was invited to participate in the World Championships of the famed Abu-Dhabi Combat Club submission grappling tournament. The ADCC grappling World Championship is the pinnacle of the no-gi professional grappling scene.

In the first round, Bravo would make his mark and pull off an upset over highly acclaimed grappler Gustavo Dantas via rear naked choke. Dantas was a talented competitor and eventually became a remarkable coach and important influencer within the jiu-jitsu community with a podcast and his business BJJ Mental Coach.

Winning at the ADCC's cements your talents as one of the top practitioners in the world. But now winning the opening round and advancing in the bracket would result in pairing up Bravo against the four-time champion and three-time ADCC champion Royler Gracie in the quarter-finals. Royler Gracie was a living legend of pure jiu-jitsu pedigree.

One of the benefits of being such a severe underdog is the basic reality that nobody expects you to win. Losing, even in the opening round, would have brought Bravo plenty of accolades and celebratory good wishes from his peer group. Losing to Royler Gracie in the quarter-finals was almost a foregone conclusion. Spectators were only tuning in to see what Royler would do to the unknown and unproven newbie. If there was any question on any of the spectators' minds, it was, "How fast was Royler going to win the match and by what technique?"

As the match started, Bravo appeared to be unusually calm and comfortable and found himself on his back with a pressing Royler Gracie on top. Bravo began working what is now well known as his half-guard lockdown, pretzeling his legs around the right leg of Royler preventing him from doing much of anything. Bravo was remaining calm underneath Royler who was trying to smash his way north towards Bravo's head. Royler appeared to be getting frustrated at his inability to move past the unorthodox and movement limiting half-guard of Bravo.

The two combatants would exchange a set of sweeps with again Bravo on his back, but this time he was able to create just enough hip movement and space to come to full guard. From full guard, it allowed Bravo to start working his "rubber guard," a very high closed guard where the legs aren't wrapped and closed around the waist of the opponent with the ankles crossed behind the hips but rather with the legs wrapped up around the back of the neck and secured with your own hands and arms. It's a technique that is contingent upon the practitioner to have incredibly flexible hips where the knees can easily rotate outward. Bravo has unbelievable hip flexibility which is a trademark and requirement of his jiu-jitsu game.

Royler was caught off guard and seemed stumped as to how to defend, counter, or escape. He attempted to tri-pod up on both his feet and drive forward, and when that proved to be ineffective, he put it in reverse and tried backing his way out of the guard. Clamping down, staying calm, and relaxed just provided Bravo with that much more time to control Royler and force him to expend a lot of energy.

Royler, now driving and posturing, forced Bravo to let go and open up his legs and arms allowing Royler to jump to the left side of Bravo who was able to retain a butterfly hook and overhook on the right side of Royler. With Royler now driving in towards Bravo and attempting to stack, Bravo punched the left arm of Royler between his legs and threw his right leg up and over the left shoulder of Royler. Before a tired and fatigued Royler realized what had just happened, Bravo had already secured a triangle choke using his legs over the shoulder and neck of Royler.

Royler quickly tried to sit back and slip out of the legs, and when that attempt failed, he quickly converted to driving in with pressure to break open the legs. It was all in vain as Bravo was now squeezing with all his might. Bravo began expending every ounce of energy he had physically while pulling the knees in tight together and pulling down on the back of the head of a gasping Royler Gracie. Then the unthinkable happened, Royler was forced to tap to avoid being choked unconscious.

As Bravo let go of the choke, a despondent Royler looked down at the mat, chin to his chest while kneeling in front of the referee who seemed to be just as surprised as everybody else in attendance. People were completely stunned at what they had just witnessed. It was Bravo who stood up and pointed towards the crowd and then began circling the mat with his arms raised as if saying, "Do you believe me now?!?!"

Bravo's impact on jiu-jitsu is undeniable. It was his expression of art that changed the way practitioners look at the sport. He was willing to be unique, distinct, break the molds, and do things his own way that set him apart. Although Bravo would lose in the next round of the ADCC tournament that year, he was awarded his black belt by Jean Jacques Machado.

Shortly thereafter, Bravo opened his very first 10th Planet Jiu-Jitsu Academy in Los Angeles, California which is based upon a no-gi jiu-jitsu system with a wide variety of Bravo specific techniques and sequences. These techniques and sequences have very "artistic," colorful, and unique names given to them and greatly diverged from the traditional norms of jiu-jitsu at the time.

"Art is never finished, only abandoned." – Leonardo da Vinci

You don't have to be Stuart Cooper or Eddie Bravo to reap the rewards of practicing the art of jiu-jitsu. Martial arts are a way to deliver fulfillment to a life worth living as you struggle to conquer your fears and grow as a person. Art is an individual way to express yourself and your unique talents. You do not have to be a famous artist to be a happy artist. You don't have to be a famous photographer to capture a great photo. Nor do you have to paint a collectible canvas to capture the heart of others or just please yourself.

Lose yourself in your art. There is an art to life, and within life, there are many forms of art. Master your art to master your life. Jiu-Jitsu is an activity that can and will transform your life if you are loyal to the success principles of jiu-jitsu. You are allowed to have your identity be associated with jiu-jitsu, not because you are the reigning, defending, undisputed king or queen of combat sports but because you have dedicated yourself to a process of personal improvement and personal transformation.

The culture of jiu-jitsu is expansive. You have practitioners that want to be dominant, or be powerful, or be superior relative to others. But when you practice the art, and by that, you truly practice the art, then jiu-jitsu is no longer a quest for dominance, or power, or superiority. It's an artistic expression of your willingness to transform yourself into a unique being, with unique talents, with unique characteristics, and be willing to share those with others in the activity and in life.

When you become an artist, a martial artist, you become a craftsman of your life. Jiu-Jitsu fans don't admire and enjoy Stuart Cooper and Eddie Bravo for their dominance, we admire them for their art and willingness to share their art with others. Artists don't hold back on their craft. They don't hold back on their creativity. They don't hold back on their efforts. Artists wake up and create because that is what artists do. They create, they construct, they transform, and then they share that art with others. You can do the same thing with your jiu-jitsu and all the other areas of your life.

Principle 19: Personal Growth

"Life is growth. If we stop growing, technically and spiritually, we are as good as dead." – Morihei Ueshiba

Many jiu-jitsu practitioners eventually ask themselves the same question, "Should I compete, or should I not compete?" Many will argue that competing is the most valuable and perhaps only way to elevate your jiu-jitsu game to your highest levels. There is no faking ability on the competition mats. You either have the skills, or you don't. The competition mats are the ultimate truth serum. You compete against others of similar rank, size, and age. How do your skills hold up against a fully resisting and offensive opponent who is also trained and prepared in the martial art?

Competition forces you to face your fears, to tax yourself mentally, and to execute techniques in a heightened state of arousal that is pure, "fight or flight." Electricity flows through your veins which can either be energetic or crippling. And the glory, what about the glory? Who doesn't dream of the glory of success in competition? Arms raised, the crowd cheering, the gold medal around your neck proving your abilities. No one can ever take away the victories of your endeavors.

Many believe that there is no way to be successful without having the proof of success behind your own competition record. You either were or were not a world champion. You either have the victories or do not have the victories. You either have the proof, or you do not have the proof. It's hard to argue with that line of thought.

But a red rose does not think of competing against the red rose next to it. The red rose just blossoms and blooms. The stars in the sky do not compete with one another. They just light up the sky. There's an old piece of wisdom that says, "If you continuously compete with others, you become bitter, but if you continuously compete with yourself, you become better."

"The only person you should ever compare yourself to is the one you used to be." – Unknown

We all have different physical attributes. We all have a different personal history with different circumstances and different desires. Not everybody is blessed with world class athletic genetics. We share the earth with over 7 billion fellow human beings. There can't be 7 billion gold medal winners even if every single one of them committed their entire lives to the pursuit of jiu-jitsu.

But the world is better with variety. We also don't want 7 billion plumbers or 7 billion doctors or 7 billion world-class guitar players. There is a path to personal success in jiu-jitsu and in life by recognizing jiu-jitsu for what it is, and that is a pathway to personal growth. Life is one big opportunity for personal growth. Some fight it, some embrace it.

What competition really offers you is just a different form of pursuing personal growth. Whether you choose that path or a different one isn't the important point. The important point is that you commit yourself to personal growth and follow the path that leads you towards your personal potential. Where that path ends nobody ever knows. We only know if we are getting closer to our potential or further away from our potential in any given endeavor.

Finding Your Path To Personal Growth and Passion

Eddie Cummings is not your typical jiu-jitsu practitioner. The small framed, messy-haired, bearded grappler is an obsessive-compulsive, over-achieving smarty-pants that has proven to be one of the most brilliant and innovative practitioners of the sport. Why would a brilliant physics student leave academia to pursue a life as a professional submission grappler?

Cummings is not a large man. He competes at 66kg's/145lbs and is 5'5" tall, although earlier in his life he weighed over 225lbs. He's a nice guy. He's quirky and intellectual, but he'll just as easily break your legs or pop your ligaments apart if you don't tap to his leg attacks in competition. He'll smile at you, but his eyes tell a deeper story. His eyes explain that he doesn't give a rat's ass of cultural or societal norms and customs. He sets his own learning path and is not tied to traditions in anything in life. He would just assume make his own traditions.

You don't meet a lot of people that drop out of high school in the ninth grade to study math and pre-med in college that led to graduate school in physics. The man is clearly intelligent. But throughout his youth and young adulthood, it seemed as if nothing offered him anything stimulating enough that could keep his focus and attention for any lasting duration of time. Yet, at his core, Cummings always had a passion for learning. Things drastically started to change once jiu-jitsu entered his life which became the outlet for laser-beam focus and dedication.

Like all jiu-jitsu practitioners, you start at the bottom as an ignorant and clueless white belt. Cummings wasn't exempt from this reality. "Newbie's" typically aren't very good especially when they lack physical traits such as size, strength, or speed. But that's the part of jiu-jitsu that was so attractive to Cummings. It was an art that would allow a person to totally control another human being with pure technical ability. Cummings would stop everything in life to dedicate himself fully to jiu-jitsu. He would either be on the mats, in front of a computer watching film, or dreaming of ways to do something better or more efficient. He is clearly a hermetic innovator. He's a mad scientist leaving some wondering of the risk that he'll turn on society after writing some bizarre quasi-intellectual manifesto about the unified theory of jiu-jitsu complete with mathematical equations.

Cummings has proved his mettle through competition. It wasn't just theoretical jiu-jitsu knowledge that he acquired. He acquired the physical skills to dominate on the mats. He is a multiple time Eddie Bravo Invitational (EBI) champion, a Polaris Super Fight winner, a Grapplers Quest Champion, and has qualified for the ADCC Championships. He is one of the finest no-Gi submission grapplers, and he's done all this through a commitment of personal growth that is astonishing.

When Cummings wanted to fully commit to jiu-jitsu, he showed up at none other than the Renzo Gracie Academy under the tutelage of John Danaher. It was Einstein meeting Einstein except Cummings was consistently bearded, and Danaher was consistently bald. Both are peculiar. Both leave observers with the belief that the two mad scientists are outside the norm of traditional social spectrums. These are not your typical New York City inhabitants who wake up on Monday mornings to don a suit and tie and board an elevator to log time in an office while chatting about the stock market.

Danaher is a perfect example of someone who has enjoyed the jiu-jitsu journey and has contributed so much to the art without being a competitor. In fact, many would argue that Danaher has contributed more to the art of jiu-jitsu than a loaded basket of multiple world champion competitors combined.

Danaher was born and raised in New Zealand. It was academics that brought him to the United States and more specifically New York City. Fate often has a funny way of evolving in the universe. Danaher was a graduate student in the Ph.D. philosophy program at Columbia University, a private Ivy League research university in Upper Manhattan. At the time in the early 1990's, Danaher was equally interested in powerlifting while working at nightclubs as a bouncer to earn extra money to support himself during his studies.

Danaher would find himself a student at the Renzo Gracie Academy during the infancy of the academy. Many would have considered him a late starter for martial arts as he didn't start practicing jiu-jitsu until he was already 28 years of age. There were very few colored belts at the academy at the time, but there were a few purple belts including Matt Serra and Ricardo Almeida, both of whom would go on to spectacular MMA careers in the UFC along with acquiring the highest levels of jiu-jitsu abilities.

It wasn't long before jiu-jitsu took over the mind of Danaher just like Eddie Cummings and so many others. Danaher would never finish his Ph.D. program at Columbia but instead would focus on doing his own research and becoming a self-directed Ph.D. in jiu-jitsu on the mats under Renzo Gracie. What sets Danaher apart from many is his systematic approach and organization to his chosen endeavors.

Danaher represents personal growth and chose to display that through his career choice in martial arts. It is highly likely that a man like Danaher could choose from many endeavors and become successful in most of them because of his systematic approach to personal improvement and growth. If there are examples of brains over brawn, it would be individuals such as Danaher and Cummings. They are students of the world. Curious. Interested. Engaged. Committed. They are passionate and obsessive compulsive about their chosen endeavors.

A Commitment To Personal Growth

Having a commitment to personal growth is a critical element of success in life. Without personal growth, you stagnate, and that stagnation is just an early form and incubation towards death. The question now is, "Why do some individuals achieve greatness while others don't? There must be something that sets humans apart.

Many would argue that greatness is born. The masses believe that greatness is genetic. The common belief is that great people are born with great and super-natural abilities that are gifts from the heavens. Reciprocally, if you lack those natural gifts, then you will never achieve greatness.

In the groundbreaking book "The Talent Code – Greatness Is Not Born It's Grown" New York Times bestselling author Daniel Coyle lays out a completely different argument. Coyle's work drew on cutting-edge neurology and research while studying talent hotbeds around the world in many different endeavors from sports, art, music, math, and business. What came from this work is a profound understanding of the importance of what is called "deep practice," a specific kind of practice that can increase learning a skill up to ten times faster than conventional practice.

When deep practice is mixed with a commitment to personal growth, the magic starts to happen. It is that passion to improve that allows your deep unconscious desires to flourish. Developing talent, growing, evolving as a person is done on a physiological level inside the mind via a microscopic neural substance in the brain called myelin. Myelin is a neural insulator that wraps around chains of nerve fibers that carry tiny electrical impulses throughout your brains circuits. Imagine rubber insulation around a wire making the signal stronger and faster by preventing the electrical impulses from leaking out.

What Danaher and Cummings have figured out, perhaps without understanding the neurology behind it, is that mixing in the intellectual with the physical during passionate practice adds skill and speed to the process. The good news about myelin and about personal growth is that it is universal. Everybody can grow myelin in their brain, and everybody can grow as an individual by understanding that skills are something that are acquired through dedicated practice and effort. Simply put, we are not static beings. We are capable of change and capable of making enormous changes within ourselves over periods of time. Where you start out isn't as important as where you finish.

Skills are acquired. Talented individuals are those who have learned the skills for success. This is not to be confused with dreaming about doing physical things professionally when you may lack the physical attributes necessary for that endeavor. What this means is that you can push yourself to experience personal growth and transform yourself into higher versions of yourself with new skills and talents. John Danaher was never a physically dominant absolute class winner at the ADCC World Championships, but his life changed forever when he dedicated himself to his preferred chosen field of study and then worked tirelessly to develop the skills and talents that made him into a teaching legend.

As you continue along your journey in jiu-jitsu and in life, imagine that there are no limitations to your future capabilities. Throw away any pre-conceived notions of what your limitations are or what you can achieve. Dream big and open yourself up to the endless possibilities that exist within your personal universe. Decide what it is you want out of your life before you put limits on what is possible.

If you want to excel at jiu-jitsu, in business, in health, in happiness, there is no need to weigh yourself down with sanctions or restrictions. You can grow towards anything, research has clearly demonstrated that. What is an essential starting point is knowing where you want to grow. What is it that you want to evolve into? Do you want to evolve into a black belt in jiu-jitsu? Do you want to evolve into a champion? Do you want to evolve into a good friend, a healthy professional, a more disciplined and organized person? Do you want to become a great parent or spouse? These are all possible through the pursuit of personal growth.

You are free to change your mind during the journey no different than Eddie Cummings or John Danaher. They may have chosen to dedicate their entire lives towards jiu-jitsu and move away from previous interests whether those were job opportunities or academics. That is what they determined was best for themselves. For you, the possibilities are endless. You may prefer to use jiu-jitsu as a stepping stone to mastery in other areas of life. Your jiu-jitsu is what you make of your jiu-jitsu. If it brings you improved discipline, then that was a success. If it delivers you more patience, then that was a success. If it teaches you to systematize your methods at work, then that was a success.

The greatest opportunity for jiu-jitsu in your life is to teach you that personal growth should be embraced with open arms and that your future possibilities are expansive. There are no limits. Many things are possible with hard work, commitment, and the sacrifices necessary to achieve your goals which will change your own life. There are no unrealistic goals, only unrealistic timelines that you set for yourself.

Commit your personal growth to paper. Write down what it is you want to become. Be specific. Imagine the possibilities. Explore the examples of others. Document what steps you are going to take to change yourself in small increments. Where do you want to be in a year from now? How about five years from now? You may end up in a place that you never imagined, but that is also a wonderful part of the journey. You may surprise even yourself with what you can become. Perhaps you can start a very successful business. Perhaps you can lose 40 pounds. Perhaps you are capable of coaching dozens of troubled and confused kids out of their uncertainty in life.

You have no idea what you are capable of until you commit yourself to the process of personal growth and look to exceed yourself. Strive for excellence and honor yourself.

"We cannot become what we want by remaining what we are." – Max Depree

Principle 20: Know Your Why?

"Never forget why you started" – Unknown

In 2008 Christian Graugart, a jiu-jitsu practitioner from Copenhagen, Denmark, was sitting at a desk asking himself some of the most important questions in life that begin with the word, "Why?" "Why am I doing this? Why am I living my life like this? Why do I have this job I hate? Why do I own this house? Why do I have all this stuff? Why am I living my life like everybody else? Why am I not happy?"

Graugart was familiar with grappling and martial arts. His father was a blackbelt in both Karate and Tae Kwon Do back in the 1970's, and martial arts was always something that resonated with him. Martial arts are often a mix between providing a purpose in life and an escape in life. They can provide focus, and they can provide a distraction. Life has a funny way of mixing us up or making us confused. Life can make us feel inadequate and insecure while we ponder all those interesting questions that begin with "why?"

In 2008, a myriad of forces was coming together for Graugart like magma under pressure beneath a volcano. Just like a volcano, eventually the pressure must be relieved, and the energy must be transferred elsewhere. A friend and training partner had just committed suicide after suffering from depression. His friend Frank was only 31 years of age. Life can make us all feel stuck and without the resources we need to fulfill our inner expectations. It's easy to imagine our destiny at either extreme of satisfaction. Some days we dream big and believe we can do something great with our lives. Other days we feel the darkness while the hopelessness infects our soul.

As we age, we tend to move like a train on railroad tracks. The tracks are set in one direction, and the momentum of the train is hard to stop. It's easy to settle along that fixed path. It's easy to stay put, grind it out, and repeat the same thing you did yesterday without giving much thought as to how your tomorrow will be any different than your yesterday.

Graugart was at an inflection point in life. He decided at that moment that he wasn't going to settle. He wasn't going to stay on those fixed train tracks. He couldn't. His heart wouldn't let him. There is no way he could let himself become trapped in his life the same way life has trapped so many others. So many others have little freedom in life along with restricted ideas as to what is possible.

Graugart was passionate about a few things; jiu-jitsu, travel, and personal freedom. He also was aware of his dislikes in life. One big issue that stood out to him was that he always disliked politics in the jiu-jitsu world where practitioners were told that they couldn't train at other academies or with other people that they wanted to train with. Graugart never understood the "us" versus "them" mindset between neighboring academies or schools. To him, jiu-jitsu is jiu-jitsu, and if you enjoy jiu-jitsu, you should be able to enjoy it with anybody and everybody else that enjoys jiu-jitsu.

By 2010 he came up with his plan. He would set off to travel the world over a five month stretch visiting as many academies and countries as he could fit in. He would document his travels on his blog richly and appropriately titled, "BJJ Globetrotter." As a brown belt, he would post his travels along with his travel desires to manage his limited budget with the approach and authentic intentions of, "Will teach jiu-jitsu for food and shelter." It was like being a hitchhiker but on a global scale. He would travel with a Gi, a pair of grappling shorts, some personal items, his phone, computer, passport, and wallet.

The trip would take him to 56 academies around the globe in 140 days and would lead to his fascinating book, "BJJ Globetrotter" which is available for free download off the website he created to document his experiences. His journey would lead to unbelievable life experiences, travel, cultures, and friendships. It would also lead to an ever-expanding organization that offers multiple jiu-jitsu training camps around the world in amazing places.

Graugart also created a community aptly named "BJJ Globetrotters," where a participant could represent any or no team in competition including IBJJF sanctioned events. Everybody is equal both on and off the mats. The overwhelming "why" to all these discoveries is to allow people an opportunity to strive to enjoy life and bring people around the world together through jiu-jitsu.

Start With "Why?"

When author and management thought leader Simon Sinek was observing leadership and success for one of his best-selling books, he noticed the importance of knowing the answer to the question, "Why?" Sinek is no stranger to success. He's a British-American author, motivational speaker, and marketing consultant to some of the largest corporations in the global economy. His insight eventually led to two breakout works of art for himself. The first was a top-selling book appropriately titled, "Start With Why." The second was a talk that he gave for the TED conference that became the third most popular TED video of all time with well over 28 million views.

TED is a nonprofit organization devoted to spreading ideas, usually in the form of short powerful talks that are 18 minutes in length or less. TED stands for Technology, Entertainment, and Design and their invited speakers provide some of the most insightful gems that help people from various disciplines and cultures acquire a deeper understanding of the world. TED.com is a clearinghouse of some of the most valuable free knowledge from the world's most inspired thinkers in our global society. When your speech becomes one of the most viewed and valued talks on TED, it speaks mountains as to the influence it has had on the world around us.

At the heart of Sinek's research is explaining how others can achieve things that seem to defy all the assumptions around their quest. Sinek would wonder, "Why is Apple so innovative during the Steve Jobs era?" They had the same access to information, talent, capital, and geographic location as other Silicon Valley companies, yet why did they prove to be far more innovative than everybody else? Why?

Or he would ask, "Why was it Martin Luther King Jr. who led the civil rights movement?" He wasn't the only man who suffered discrimination in a pre-civil rights society. So why him? Why was it the Wright Brothers who figured out how to fly an airplane on the beach in North Carolina? There were other teams that had better talent and had far more financial funding.

What Sinek discovered is that there is a pattern to success when it comes to thinking, acting, and communicating. Top level individuals or teams all do it similarly. He calls his concept the "Golden Circle" where in the center is the bullseye which he describes as the "Why." The next outer circle is the "How" and finally the outer circle is the "What." Everybody on the planet should be able to figure out and describe "what" they do daily whether you are an individual, a business, or an institution. Some can then go on to describe in detail "how" they do things because they are self-aware and took time to think about their individual processes of how they do things.

What Sinek really discovered is that few people or organizations can really describe or understand "why" they are doing something. Why are they doing what they are doing? And the answer shouldn't be describing a result such as making a profit. Making a profit may be a positive and welcome result of efforts and actions, but making a profit is rarely a deep reason why humans or organizations accomplish something great.

The "Why" in the question is really the purpose. It's the inner motivation. It's the reason you are going to push through all the hardships and obstacles along the way. What is your calling? What is your belief? What is your purpose? These all add up to your "why?" Why are you going to work hard? Why are you going to be a jiu-jitsu practitioner? Why are you going to train every week? Why are you going to show up when you don't feel like it? Why are you going to make the right decisions on your nutrition? Why are you going to get enough sleep? Why are you going to help others?

Inspired and successful individuals start with "why?" Then they move outwards to "how?" and then finally "what?" But it makes no sense to them to expend a ton of energy on something, anything for that matter, if they can't clearly justify it to themselves as to "why?" We can justify any of our actions based on logic and reason. We can justify any of our actions based on our feelings and emotions at the time of the decision. But our inner gut and heart will have the most impact on our "why." If we deep down know why we are doing something, because of its deep meaning to us while we are on the journey, then we can set ourselves on the path to success with confidence and conviction for at that point, we know our "why." Everything after the why just becomes a logistical issue.

A Human Energy Field

Sometimes you pick your endeavors, and sometimes your endeavors pick you. Such was the case with Renzo Gracie. Renzo is as pure bred as they come in jiu-jitsu lineage. He is the grandson of Carlos Gracie Sr. and trained under the instruction of Rolls Gracie and Carlos Gracie Jr. Renzo, like many of his family members, was more than just jiu-jitsu. He was a fighter and a damn good one at that. He was very much a fighter like his cousin Rickson, another amazing legend in martial arts history, who used jiu-jitsu as part of his arsenal to take on any and all challengers in no-holds-barred fighting around the world, often against men much bigger physically than themselves.

Renzo may be more inclined to say, "jiu-jitsu picked me." He knows his roots, his family tree, the family legacy. His father brought him into this world as a Gracie jiu-jitsu fighter and ever since being an infant has dedicated his life to pursuing the combat martial arts. Why jiu-jitsu for Renzo? Because Renzo is jiu-jitsu and jiu-jitsu is Renzo. It's in his blood. It's in his DNA. He knows his purpose, his passion, his calling.

Renzo would go on to move permanently to the United States and away from Brazil. You would not expect such a tough and fearless fighter to be so personable. Yet, behind the bruising brawn and willingness to fight anyone at any time, is one of the most charismatic individuals in sports. He'll light up a room with his energy. You know when Renzo is present. You don't just see him, you feel his presence. His aura has a very strong energy field. He is gracious, funny, warm, compassionate, and full of human life. He'll light up your spirits and make you feel as though nature has touched your soul.

Renzo has brought the highest level of jiu-jitsu to New York City at the famed Renzo Gracie Academy. The Renzo Gracie Academy is home to world class instructors like John Danaher along with students that have reached the pinnacle levels of the sport. He has provided a church for those who want to dedicate their lives in pursuit of their own "why." Why jiu-jitsu? Because for some, jiu-jitsu is life itself. It is their spirit, their profession, their hobby, their purpose, and their reason for working so hard on the mats. Jiu-jitsu is the purpose for their lives.

Living in New York City and training at a facility like the Renzo Gracie Academy allows individuals to associate daily with people who share the same beliefs. They all share the common belief which is, "jiu-jitsu is their purpose." None of the students need to justify anything to each other. What is known need not be discussed. There is no explanation needed between each other as to why they spend so much time on the mats. There is no need to rationalize why they spend so much time in pursuit of the practice. They just get to show up and train and share the experience with one another.

As you proceed through life, you'll find that some people do things just for the money with the belief that the money will allow them the opportunity to do what they really want to do in life. You will also come across people from time to time that take the opposite approach which is, "I'm going to do what I really want to do in life, and the money may or may not follow." But they don't change their behaviors and actions because they are already doing what it is that they feel they are supposed to be doing with their lives. They already know their own personal "why?"

When you acknowledge your "why" in life, you don't wait for invitations or signs from the sky. You don't ask your parents what they think you ought to do or wonder what your neighbor might say. You don't do it to impress your high school friends or to create another bullet point on your resume. You do things because you know what it is you want to do, and then you just go and do it regardless of how hard it is or how long it might take you to achieve your goals. When you know your "why" you don't wait for permission from others because nobody could stop you from doing what it is you want to do anyway, so there is no need for permission. You follow your "why" because you believe in the mission at the core of your existence. Your belief in purpose is what keeps you on the path regardless of how strange or different your purpose is from others around you.

Your belief is what brings you meaning. When you know what your "why" is and why you do what you do, even the toughest days and biggest obstacles aren't going to stop you from moving forward and carrying on your mission. Your days become easier regardless of setbacks. When you look at the examples set by Christian Graugart, the founder of BJJ Globetrotters or Renzo Gracie, you witness people that strongly know their personal "why." They are unstoppable in their personal journey and have clarity of thought on their purpose and intentions.

Principle 21: Perseverance

"With ordinary talent and extraordinary perseverance, all things are attainable." – Thomas Fowell Buxton

It was once said, "To begin is for everyone. To persevere is for saints." There is nothing exceptional that can be accomplished if quitting is part of the curriculum. Hardship, failure, and frustrations are all certainties while on the path to success. If there is one thing that will test you in jiu-jitsu and in life, it's your perseverance.

Towering over his students in a quaint and beautiful commercial real estate space with jiu-jitsu mats is Paulo Ribeiro, an oversized and tall bearded man with an infectious and contagious smile but a demeanor more like a gentle giant. Ribeiro, a fourth-degree black belt, has been a black belt in jiu-jitsu for more than a decade and a half. Jiu-Jitsu and judo have been his life's work. It's his career. It is his purpose.

Ribeiro runs his own academy like the patriarch of a tight-knit family in Naples, Florida catering to a more distinguished and socially affluent student body. Naples is a beautiful city, set in the Southwest section of Florida directly on the Gulf of Mexico. It is known for high-end shopping and exquisite golf courses. If you didn't know any better, you might believe you are in Nice, France or some other high-end and elite community with the architecture, the wealth, the yachts, the mansions, and the high-end automobiles. Yet, even here in the center of world-class culture and sophisticated dining, jiu-jitsu is present. Jiu-jitsu has now penetrated itself into most corners of the world and across most social demographics.

Jiu-jitsu is Paulo Ribeiro's passion. He's on the mats teaching, on the mats refereeing, and still on the mats competing at IBJJF events. But on this day, he is reminding his students once again of one of his favorite sayings, "Jiu-Jitsu exists to make you quit!"

Anybody can start practicing jiu-jitsu. There are no precursors or prerequisites. You can come to the mats and train. It's fun. It's social. It's brain teasing. It's rolling around and getting in a non-boring workout. But Ribeiro knows the truth, jiu-jitsu exists to make you quit. Most will quit within a few weeks or even a few months. Some will make it 18 months and maybe earn their blue belt. Then they will vanish, never to be seen on the mats again.

The Science Of Grit

When you start any new endeavor, it's always exciting, fresh, and new. Everything is new. Learning is fast because you are starting with nothing at ground zero. After a short while the novelties wear off, and you don't learn new things at the same breakneck pace. It's a grinding path forward only accomplished through perseverance.

It's unlikely that you will ever know your limits or your potential in jiu-jitsu, just like in most endeavors in life. There is no way of knowing what those limits are unless you apply yourself over the long-term and persevere through the obstacles that present themselves along the way. That's exactly what was discovered by the researcher and bestselling author Angela Duckworth.

Duckworth was a math teacher and graduate of Harvard College before heading to study psychology and popular science at the University of Oxford for her master's degree in addition to the University of Pennsylvania for her Ph.D. doctorate program. As a teacher and as a student, she began to realize that the most successful students weren't always the ones who were the smartest or had the most natural ability. The word that she began to use to describe the difference between individual students was the word 'grit' which she believed was a combination of passion and perseverance and the person's willingness to apply those characteristics towards a singular but important personal goal. She went so far during her studies to come up with a proprietary grit scale which is used as a predictive measuring tool when assessing the likelihood of success in individuals in a wide range of applications.

Duckworth used her grit scale to predict success outcomes ranging from West Point graduates to winners in the National Spelling Bee. Duckworth would be named a MacArthur "genius" in 2013 for her work on 'grit' which she went on and published her findings and research in the highly acclaimed book, "Grit: The Power of Passion and Perseverance."

Duckworth's research was not only revolutionizing but fascinating because her lab found that her grit scale methods of measurement was more predictive on success than other methods such as I.Q. scores or SAT scores used by large numbers of institutions for recruiting and selection purposes. Unfortunately, grit cannot be applied to all individuals in all situations. You cannot force yourself to be interested in something that you are not naturally interested in. But if you are interested in something, you can apply personal grit in ways to develop and deepen not only your interest in the subject but advance the acquisition of skills in that endeavor. If you can incubate and foster the genuine interest, then you can apply yourself towards the difficult and frustrating practice that it takes to excel in it and make you successful at it. It is the grit that helps you maintain a sense of hope and resilience in the face of failures, setbacks, and obstacles.

An Incubating Spider-Ninja

There's so much importance to perseverance in jiu-jitsu and in life. There are so many times that you will want to quit just before a breakthrough was set to happen or your life was about to change. Nobody knows this more than Mike Bidwell who is now known as the "Spider-Ninja." Mike is a jiu-jitsu black belt under Phil Migliarese and Ken Kronenberg. He's a popular instructor, YouTuber, blogger, and leader of his BJJafter40 online community of followers. What makes Bidwell so unique, even in jiu-jitsu circles, was the 13 years he spent as a brown belt before finally being promoted to black belt.

In 2012 and now over the age of 40, Bidwell was ready to pack it in and quit jiu-jitsu for good. A brown belt since 2001, he went on and gained a lot of weight, was out of shape, and his skills were less than sharp for his belt rank. Bidwell would explain what happened next, "I asked myself how I would ever explain this to my children and more importantly to myself. The thought of living with the fact that I just gave up was unbearable. So I got just a little bit of momentum going, and that momentum turned into more and more. So sometimes you need to be pushed a little, and that momentum can quickly turn to inspiration. Then when inspiration becomes a conviction, you cannot be stopped."

The symptoms of spiraling downward and being stuck in a rut are familiar with many. First, you start eating poorly, which is bad enough when you aren't training an adequate amount. But when injuries come calling and your physical activities plummet, the poor nutrition is a proven recipe for failure.

It became a vicious cycle for Bidwell. Injuries led to stress, stress led to food, poor physical conditioning morphed into a poor emotional and mental state, and soon enough he was in a multi-year funk where his skills stalled. Terrible digestion problems and Irritable Bowel Syndrome just complicated matters. At times there were not just weeks, but months where he didn't train. It was a human unravelling in what often seemed like an inescapable downward spiral. It was a spiritual black hole where the gravity force seemed too strong to escape from.

He arrived at a breaking point. He was either going to have to make radical adjustments or just quit altogether and wallow in the failure for the rest of his life. He sought out advice from some respected friends and mentors from the jiu-jitsu community, and he made the commitment to at least try and get into better physical shape. At least that would improve his life in many ways. Bidwell would overhaul his entire eating and nutritional system and switched to an almost pure plant-based diet. Better nutrition meant better recovery and better energy levels. Positive momentum was soon building within his daily routines. Alas, he turned the corner.

After losing fifty pounds and committing himself to his jiu-jitsu practice, Bidwell pulled an entire 180-degree turn in his life. The prestigious black belt was given to Bidwell by his longtime mentor Ken Kronenburg in January of 2014, and soon the Spider-Ninja was sharing his experiences on social media and YouTube building a loyal following with his BJJAfter40 content.

It was jiu-jitsu that offered Bidwell a chance to gain better clarity and perspective into his own life. For Bidwell, jiu-jitsu has become a quest towards dissolving the ego and getting to know his own true self and living in that vibration. Jiu-jitsu has been a path to personal enlightenment for Bidwell where he loses a sense of time, learning how to be in the moment on the mats when he is with others.

Those that practice jiu-jitsu can find the humor in the description of jiu-jitsu as, "the gentle art." It may sound gentle, and the principles of success may sound gentle, but anybody that practices the art will tell you first hand that the art is never completely gentle. It is a physical endeavor that combines attributes of technique, mobility, flexibility, strength, power, speed, and shear willpower at times. Those physical requirements may be daunting to those who are well past their youth and especially well into adulthood. These became realities for Bidwell, and they will become realities for you on your quest.

Mike Bidwell has carved out a loyal following of practitioners over the age of 40. Bidwell has physical characteristics that are unique. He's a very flexible guy. He's very creative and can now contort himself into some amazing positions while rolling with others.

What If You Are Older And Inflexible?

Being an older athlete with awesome flexibility isn't a reality for many adult practitioners and especially those who are over the age of 40. That's where Stephen Whittier of SBG (Straight Blast Gym) lends his experience and wisdom.

Whittier has his own cult-like following in his '40PlusBJJ' community that he developed and groomed over the years. His followers are global, loyal, and very appreciative of what Whittier has brought to those who want to enjoy practicing the art of jiu-jitsu but have grown to be "age-challenged." Being an older practitioner usually means there are physical limitations associated with being an aging athlete. 40PlusBJJ is dedicated to the unique tactical and technical needs of jiu-jitsu practitioners who don't have the same physical qualities and characteristics of those in their physical prime that still can train at a higher output level.

Whittier is a unique blend of a very relatable guy who you would just as much look forward to going out and have a beer with along with him being a full-on martial arts bad-ass. He's an intellect at heart, a not-so-unusual commonality amongst many high-level practitioners. Jiu-jitsu is certainly a physical activity. But it's also an intellectual endeavor which is why many smarty-pants find the activity so appealing. Whittier is no different. To think that he ended up as one of the highest-level martial arts instructors in the world should come as no surprise. He simply combined two of his core skills; a love for combat and a love for teaching.

To start, Whittier had a very distinguished academic career in "the real world" (the place that exists off the mats so to speak.) He graduated Summa Cum Laude and was a member of Phi Beta Kappa. He was a Wheaton Scholar at Wheaton College in Massachusetts, his home state where he still resides. He attended Tufts University on a full academic scholarship and continued as a teacher for four additional years as a lecturer in the English Department.

Whittier has dedicated decades of his life to the study of the martial arts earning advanced belts and credentials in jiu-jitsu, Muay Thai, kickboxing, mixed-martial-arts, and Jeet Kune Do. His skills are of the highest caliber. High-level practitioners understand the level of ability required to reach a black belt in jiu-jitsu and the years of mat time that it takes to achieve that level of competence and skill. Whittier, for all his skills in jiu-jitsu, is of even a higher caliber in the sport of Muay Thai. In fact, in the spring of 2018 Whittier became one of only four people ever to be promoted to the rank of Red Mongkol in Sityodtong Muay Thai kickboxing under the legendary Sityodtong USA Director and coach Mark DellaGrotte.

Whittier looks more like a corporate executive than a combat expert who is a lethal killing machine. He is a perfect example of someone that has learned life skills that allowed him to excel in martial arts and inversely, learned skills in martial arts that allowed him to excel in life and business. Whittier is a highly successful entrepreneur, author, consultant, and owner of Whittier International, LLC a consulting firm that focuses on helping other skilled entrepreneurs to develop and scale their service-based businesses. This is on top of being the owner of SBG East Coast in Wareham, Massachusetts, one of the premier martial arts training centers in the entire world.

What sets Whittier apart from so many others? Perseverance. The man never gives up. When he puts his mind to something, he bites down on it like a shark to a dead fish carcass. There is no prying something away from him. He is unrelenting in his daily disciplines to learn, grow, and share his knowledge.

Life is full of setbacks, obstacles, and reasons to quit. You can quit the education process. You can quit running your own company. You can quit a diet that will make you better. You can quit playing the guitar, or you can quit your pursuit of jiu-jitsu. The reality is, when you quit, nobody else ends up caring. They probably prefer you to quit for their own competitive advantages and ego. Nobody will end up caring except you. Perseverance is that inner grit that keeps you going when you want to quit or feel justified in quitting.

Make no mistake, there are plenty of ways to justify quitting. You are tight on time. You lack the appropriate financial resources. You may not have supporting cast members in the story of your life. You may not feel you are gifted athletically. Your body hurts. The reasons for quitting are countless. But you can't quit. Actually, you can quit. The question is, "Will you quit?" That's up to you. That's dependent on how bad you want something. How bad are you willing to work for it? How patient are you with the realistic length of time that it takes to achieve any of life's worthwhile goals?

"Great works are performed not by strength but by perseverance." – Samuel Johnson

Principle 22: Longevity

"There is no such thing as great work without longevity." – Johnny Hunt

Jiu-Jitsu, like many arts, has an interesting way of attracting interesting and unique individuals. There are men and women. Big and small. Flexible, powerful, skinny, and weak. There is also the old and the young. And each practitioner is slightly different than the rest in their own inimitable way. Then there are the personalities of the practitioners. That just opens an entirely new box of fascinating qualities amongst jiu-jitsu participants with an additional wide range of personal attributes spanning from totally weird to downright brilliant.

Each unique individual in the sport of jiu-jitsu brings their own set of skills, attributes, and contributions to the sport and the social spectrum. Some practitioners have been around for so long that they have seen this human diversity phenomenon over long periods of time and at the same time contribute to the diverse sub-culture themselves. One such example of a very unique athlete is Alexandre "Xande" Ribeiro.

"Xande" which is pronounced "Shawn-Dee" in his native Portuguese, is like a human Energizer Bunny. He just keeps going and going.

With a clean-shaven head, a well-built physique, dead-pan eyes, but a smile that could light up a room, Xande is one of the few top-level competitive athletes that has stood the test of time. He's Mr. Clean with a vicious guillotine (and one heck of a cross collar choke).

Xande began training jiu-jitsu at the young age of 10 in Manaus, Brazil and began competing shortly after that, losing less than a handful of times during his progression through all the lower ranking belt promotions.

By 1999 at the age of 18, Xande would move to Rio de Janeiro to study law and would continue his jiu-jitsu training by joining forces with his brother Saulo, who was also a fantastic and successful competitor. It would be Saulo Ribeiro that would go on to write and publish the highly popular and bestselling instructional book, "Jiu-Jitsu University" in 2008 that remains a must have resource for every jiu-jitsu practitioner to this day.

In 2001, ten years into his training and at the age of 20, Xande was awarded his black belt and began competing against the very best guys in the world.

In competition, Xande could be described as a stone-cold cerebral assassin. Xande quickly began earning victories against a who's who list in elite grappling competitions such as Pablo Popovitch, Jeff Monson, Erik Paulson, Dean Lister, Eduardo Telles, Marcelo Garcia, Robert Drysdale, Braulio Estima, Roberto Abreu, and Andre Galvao. As the victories stacked up, so did the titles and accolades. Xande is a multiple time IBJJF

World Champion, IBJJF Pan-American Champion, IBJJF World No-Gi Champion, and a two-time ADCC Champion.

There is an amazing physical accomplishment of Xande. Almost two decades after receiving his black belt, he is still competing at the highest level of competition. He possesses an extremely high level of proficiency in his competitive jiu-jitsu game and is a well-rounded grappler. But for all his skills and talents, he is best known for his unbelievable guard retention abilities. In 25 years of competition, only two competitors have passed his guard. Jiu-jitsu practitioners around the world should let that sink in for a moment. As of 2018, his guard hasn't been passed in 11 years.

Xande puts a lot of focus and attention on his pursuit of longevity in life and in jiu-jitsu. His approach is to keep evolving and be smart with the physical requirements of the sport. That means having a jiu-jitsu game that is perfect for every age of his life. Xande stays physically fit. He eats optimally with clean and healthy nutrition. He's muscular but lean. He is a healthy individual both on and off the mats.

While it is impressive to be a Xande or Saulo Ribeiro on the competition scene, it is important to understand and assess why you are training jiu-jitsu and what it is that you want to accomplish in life. The way you approach training, business, or life must align with your goals and values. Sure, jiu-jitsu training can be a great workout. You can push the pace, use your muscles explosively and powerfully, break a sweat, and train hard. But jiu-jitsu is an art and an aid to the bigger picture in life. It's a gateway to personal excellence. Winning world championships isn't in everybody's future. Nor is the pursuit of elite championships a pathway to a fun and healthy life for most practitioners.

For most jiu-jitsu practitioners, the focus should be on longevity, which not only includes longevity in jiu-jitsu but more importantly longevity in life. Jiu-jitsu should only be one of the many gateways to peak performance to enhance and maximize your life experiences. This should continue as you age, mature, obtain additional wisdom, and then hopefully get to use all the accumulated wisdom and experience within your life. What this essentially means is that through the portal of jiu-jitsu, your individual life becomes better year after year as you progress along your journey. While your physical abilities may slowly diminish over time, your overall success in life should continue to increase.

This continuous life enhancement protocol towards health and personal excellence will only be possible through a commitment to longevity. You may not maintain the exact physical abilities that you had when you were 20, or 25, or even 35, but the experience and wisdom that you pick up during your journey will allow you the capacity to obtain higher levels of personal achievement with each passing year. To progress through a lifetime of jiu-jitsu and a lifetime of 'normal life' while staying strong, healthy, and energetic isn't about luck. It is about paying attention to what matters, what doesn't, and then doing the work with dedication and discipline to proceed according to plan.

When it comes to jiu-jitsu, there are many youthful practitioners who think about dominating in the sport or physically dominating another human in life. That is their age and ego talking. In turn, when they show up to class, their objective is to always dominate their opponent, regardless of long-term consequences. They often risk injury to either themselves or to their training partners in their quest for temporary superiority. These often are the same individuals who will ignore proven principles of life success such as getting enough rest, sleep, eating properly, avoiding drugs and alcohol, and living a low stress lifestyle.

When you practice jiu-jitsu, you should establish the following priorities in the correct order of importance; safety, fun, learning, and then perhaps winning. This isn't what happens for a vast selection of typical practitioners. As a result, many practitioners find themselves in a negative feedback loop that includes the following chain of events; train too hard, compete, get injured, make use of a doctor. The doctor will usually prescribe either physical therapy or surgery. Surgery leads to more rehabilitation and therapy. In a rush to return to the mats, they start training again too quickly, resuming training that is too much volume and too intense in quality. They get injured again. Back to Mr. or Mrs. MD sports doctor or orthopedic. Begin the therapy or resort to additional surgeries. Finally, they have enough of the nonsense and quit the practice of jiu-jitsu permanently, blaming injuries and physical limitations as the reasons for their permanent exit.

Jiu-jitsu is indeed a portal to a healthier lifestyle and better quality of life off the mats through discipline and a focus on longevity. This means an overall more enjoyable life. It means a more satisfying life. It means a more fulfilling life that includes friends, health, challenge, confidence, vitality, and the acquisition of problem solving skills that are valuable in other important areas of life. Indeed, we all have physical peaks that typically diminish too early for most of us. We also have mental peaks which occur much later in life. If you play your cards right, you can stay healthy and fit well into your 60's, 70's and far beyond which allows you to utilize your mental fitness to navigate and achieve the pleasures of life.

As you have discovered already, life brings with it a lot of physical, emotional, and mental pains. You've been dealing with pains most of your adult life. Jiu-jitsu is supposed to be a remedy and a conduit to less pain, not more pain. If your life is more painful because of jiu-jitsu, then you may be doing it wrong. Sure, after hard practices, you should experience some soreness, no different than if you were weightlifting for gains or running in preparation for a marathon. There is a fine line between legitimate pain and soreness though and you do not want to cross it.

The purpose of life is not to instill as much pain as possible in all keys areas. Your health is not supposed to be painful. Your relationships are not supposed to be painful. Your job and career are not supposed to be painful. You will not achieve anything worthy without some blood, sweat, and tears but the intensity and discipline that you bring to your daily routine should never have a negative impact on your long-term health and well-being.

Many traditional sports preach the endless pursuit of more intensity. They encourage more strength and conditioning, harder training sessions, longer training sessions, or more training sessions. If some training is good, then double or triple that level is extra good. Although more training certainly has benefits, there are points where the laws of diminishing returns set in and more harm than good is resulting from the increase in total workload. This also applies to all areas of life.

Being at the office and working hard is good. Working more yields more results. But taken to an extreme, any individual that eats, sleeps, and works all their waking hours entirely in the office is not living a happy life nor a healthy life. It's too much mental pounding day after day. Pains will begin to surface, it's just a matter of where, how much, and how intense.

Most people including those who have achieved greater than average success in some areas of life will follow the same systematic approach to pain and suffering. They will push themselves past the brink and then look for remedies to escape those pains such as food, alcohol, drugs, and other escape mechanisms. It's this typical model and way of thinking that can be damaging to your long-term well-being that works against a longevity model for success. There are alternatives to the "go-crazy until you burn out" mentality. Life doesn't all have to be about short-term gains at the expense of long-term pain and suffering.

Jiu-jitsu should be one of the great joys and opportunities of your life. It should not be the source of strain, constant pounding, and breakdown until you are so broken that you can't get out of bed in your 40's (or sooner). You must take a preventative approach to injuries that can occur in jiu-jitsu and in life in general. Jiu-jitsu is a privilege in life. Nobody is forcing you to do it. You don't "have" to do it, you "get" to do it. But as you will see by showing up at your academy over time, the grind of training and the grind of life will punish many participants and inflict so much pain and suffering that it strips out all the joy in their day to day routine.

Living with longevity as an intended purpose requires a non-traditional lifestyle and mental approach compared to the normal person. Keep in mind, most Americans in the United States are on track for one form of chronic disease or another with the rest of the world seemingly anxious to follow suit. Heart disease, cancer, diabetes, high blood pressure, elevated cholesterol levels, obesity, mental illness, depression, loneliness, and financial problems are just an expected part of life for most people. It does not have to be this way if you focus on health and longevity as part of your core living mandate.

When you approach jiu-jitsu and other areas of your life through a longevity based looking glass, you will begin to see how the choices that others make end up being detrimental and harmful to their own long-term self-interest. The difference between health and happiness versus sickness and anxiety includes the core foundations of human performance. What you eat and drink matters. How much you sleep matters. How much stress you have in your life matters. How much you exercise matters. How much you use your brain and learn in life matters. How much social interaction you have with quality human beings matters.

"Take care of your body. It's the only place you have to live." – Jim Rohn

Improvements in life come over time. The same applies in jiu-jitsu. It takes time to improve, yet between a combination of impatience and unrealistic expectations, many practitioners quit jiu-jitsu because they either become injured too often or they become too frustrated with their progress and quit. This often requires them to start all over again in a new endeavor and repeat their personal madness. Time is your friend in jiu-jitsu if you are doing it correctly. You should be enjoying your time on the mats. You should be enjoying your friends that you see at practice. You should be enjoying living a healthier lifestyle through the exercise provided by jiu-jitsu. You should be enjoying each belt rank along the path to a lifetime of jiu-jitsu.

Think of jiu-jitsu like baking a cake. You could have all the right ingredients and assemble them in the right order, but you still must wait for the cake to bake. 2 minutes at 1,000 degrees isn't the same as 45 minutes at 350 degrees. Things don't work that way.

"No matter how great the talent or efforts, some things just take time. You can't produce a baby in one month by getting nine women pregnant." – Warren Buffett

It is typical and natural to want to be promoted to black belt as quickly as possible, often at the speed of light. If you are a lifetime practitioner though, belt rank starts to lose importance the higher your rank. Why? At that point, belt color or rank more adequately describes "time" in the endeavor of jiu-jitsu. A higher-ranking belt holder is just a dedicated practitioner that discovered and started training jiu-jitsu earlier than you did and didn't quit.

Stop and imagine how amazing the current members of your academy would be if all of them learned to avoid injury and stay healthy not just for two years or five years but for ten years, twenty years, or forty years? How much knowledge would they have acquired over the decades? How much fun would they have had and how healthy would they be if they just put themselves in a position to keep going rather than having to quit?

Health leads to productivity in other areas of life. There is a real downside of premature declining health (and premature death that was self-induced through poor lifestyle choices). Likewise, there is a real upside to extending your health that leads to a fulfilling life of longevity. As you know, life is hard, but life can get much easier if you build it on a platform of personal excellence. Over time, all those consistent small improvements that you have been making turn into a bountiful bundle of success. Wouldn't it be nice to reap the rewards for an extended duration throughout your lifetime?

Jiu-jitsu ability is greatly enhanced through durability. Durability will lead to a much better and efficient personal game of jiu-jitsu. Each time you roll you log information in your brain. Over the years, you will have the opportunity to log all this experience in problem solving and pattern recognition into your subconscious. Your ability to adapt to change is crucial as jiu-jitsu will continue to evolve. But after years and years of practice, you will have seen (and felt) so many situations and scenarios that exist on the grappling mats.

Coaches, mentors, and learning aids are important, but experience is critical. The ability to combine experience with a healthy body and a healthy mind will create a better jiu-jitsu practitioner and a more productive person in life. Sustained peak performance is built upon a platform of longevity.   A longevity outlook isn't just about one thing. Longevity and success aren't about changing a habit or two in your life. Longevity will evolve so that it is your life. It will be a life of commitment, discipline, and a process of improvement.

Your practice of jiu-jitsu and your life should not be two separate things. They are one thing. Everything is part of your life and should be treated as such. Your work, your family, your health, your finances, and your happiness are all part of the greater composition of you as an individual. Learn from mentors and role models in the jiu-jitsu community like Xande and Saulo Ribeiro. How are they living their life? What are they doing to enhance their health and wellness? How did jiu-jitsu lead them to such a fulfilling and stimulating life on and off the mats? They are following a longevity model of success backed by proven principles.

Conclusion

As you proceed in your jiu-jitsu journey, be cautious about having a mindset that your jiu-jitsu will have a shelf-life with an expiration date. You will see so many others come and go in a relatively short period of time. Some of them may be quite athletic and may have experienced success in competition at high levels. But you don't really want to take that approach where you take up jiu-jitsu for a relatively short period of time and then eventually flame out.

Keep your eyes focused on the future and what you will do next as you allow jiu-jitsu to mold you as a person. The journey isn't about just becoming a great temporary athlete. It's not about being the best in competition for a split moment in time. Mastering jiu-jitsu is the portal into becoming a remarkable person. The long-term journey of mastering the art is about the personal transformation that spills over into other areas of your life. Learning jiu-jitsu will require you to learn the way of success. You will have to learn and implement key principles if you are to succeed in jiu-jitsu and it is these same principles that are useful in other areas in life.

Do you want to be the person who later in life refers to jiu-jitsu as something that you did, "back then?" Or do you want to be the person who keeps moving forward on personal self-mastery while attaining greater personal achievements? When you focus on the future progress of your journey in jiu-jitsu and in life you can use all your accumulating experiences as building blocks to transform yourself into the person that you seek to become.

Here's the reality about the journey that you have now put yourself on. If you want to be good at jiu-jitsu, if you really want to "master" jiu-jitsu based upon your own personal characteristics and potential, you'll have to miss out on some other things. You'll miss some comfort and junk food because you want to be healthy and train. You'll miss some good drink because you will want to be healthy and train. You will miss some social time with people that aren't associated with the jiu-jitsu lifestyle because you must either choose to live clean or be impacted by negative influences. But in the end, you will make progress on what you want in life. The balance will naturally evolve as you strike those middle grounds.

Jiu-jitsu is a very practical martial art. It's arguably one of the most effective martial arts. You have learned that the principles required to succeed in learning such an art are the same principles that must be applied to succeed in most areas of life. Learn the way of one thing, and you learn the way for all things.

These principles are tried and true. They stand the test of time. They were applicable a thousand years ago, and they will be applicable a thousand years from now. You will end up exercising your brain, your body, and your soul. You will make new social contacts. You will become stronger. You will become more flexible. You will gain confidence. You will learn how to compete in stressful situations either in practice or in actual competition. These are core life skills.

You will fail, repeatedly. Occasionally you will get physically hurt or experience pain, and that will prepare you for life. Life itself will hurt you. You will age either way, and life can break your body. Life can also break your heart. Become resilient. Become pliable. There is no faking it in jiu-jitsu just like there really is no faking it in real life. When you look in the mirror, you will see who you really are at any moment in time.

Nobody is telling you that jiu-jitsu will be easy even with the proven principles of success. It won't be easy for you, and it wasn't easy for anybody else who dedicated themselves in the past to the art that they dearly love. Jiu-jitsu will always remain problem solving under pressure. That is just more preparation for life. Your nose must be quickly introduced to Mr. Grindstone if you are to have any shot at success in life.

For now, you may only own a few pairs of shoes, a single gi, and a rash guard. All your possessions may fit into a 10-foot by 10-foot room. But if you practice something that resonates with your soul, you will feel rich. You will have spent the most energetic years of your life testing your physical, mental, and emotional capacities in pursuit of a dream and a lifestyle. You will have proven to yourself that with lots of hard work, doing what you love with others who share the same love will never feel inadequate.

You may not ever become the best guard player or the most credentialed competitor. You may not achieve the highest of the highest ranks, or be the most feared on the mats, but following your dream and your heart will teach you that happiness and self-love don't come down to being the very best relative to others. Happiness and self-love come down to pursuing your own goals and dreams and connecting with your own soul on that journey through your communities and the world around you.

As with many decisions you will need to make in your life, you will need to figure out what is true in your life and what is worth pursuing. Not everybody will agree with your decisions or choose jiu-jitsu as a pathway to self-improvement. You will always struggle to make the best decisions for yourself, and you will still make mistakes throughout your lifetime. You will need to think for yourself unless you want a life that is directed by others. Then you must have the courage to execute on the items that you decide are best for you.

Time is always moving. There is nothing you could do to get back time or slow down time. Therefore, your time should be spent on pursuing the things that you find to be the most meaningful along with doing those things with people that create the most positive relationships with your pursuits.

As you quickly learned during your first few times to the mats, jiu-jitsu will force you to deal with reality. There is no faking success on the mats. You can either execute techniques against a resisting opponent, or you can't. Life is like that as well. Long-term, you can't fake success in your internal world. You are either finding fulfillment in your life, or you aren't. These internal truths will emerge over other items such as what you temporarily own or what your current job title is.

Jiu-jitsu will help you deal with reality. You must develop a deep understanding and acceptance of this reality.

You must accept the combat art for what it is and not what you wish it were in your life. You have your dreams, and when you interject those dreams within reality with determination and persistence, success will eventually emerge on the other side. On and off the mats you will be presented with problems to solve, with limited time to solve those problems. During that problem-solving engagement, you will make mistakes, and your weaknesses will be exposed. How you deal with these realities is what will determine your outcomes in life.

The harsh reality is, mastering jiu-jitsu is hard. Mastering yourself is hard. Navigating life is hard. How you deal with the psychological puzzles in your daily life can either help or hurt you in life. Learning how to use a technique or defend against a technique will help you learn and implement other techniques or defend against new attacks. Dealing with problems and moving past the pain of failures is what will bring you the rewards and pleasure of the experience. If it were easy, it wouldn't be so satisfying.

It's inspirational to see others who have similar goals that have experienced many of the same problems and struggles as us. Nobody else is exempt from the pain of failure. It's just that some people have the inner drive to evolve past their problems and struggles. This required them to identify the root causes of their problems and struggles so that appropriate solutions could be identified and implemented. Only by facing their realities were they able to design alternatives that allowed them to do the work that was required to achieve their objectives. They all had to do the work.

As you develop your skills, you will reach greater heights. This will encourage you to chase bigger goals that lead to even greater heights. From time to time failing at these higher levels and heights may be more painful as you have further to fall. This is all part of a successful life.

Setbacks will be part of your journey. Overcoming your setbacks will be required to move past your failures. Every person will have setbacks, will suffer losses, or lose something that they think they cannot live without. Your health will go through cycles. Your finances will be volatile from time to time. You may even find yourself at a point where you believe your entire life is ruined and there is nothing positive ahead. But these are all cycles within our lives. Every phase of life eventually comes and goes. You don't stay a baby forever. Nor are you in high school forever. Broken hearts mend themselves over time, and business opportunities come and go.

You can have a very safe life if you stay in place. Staying in place will ultimately prove to be boring, yet there will be comfort from being predictable as nothing changes. Or you can take the risk and have a much better life albeit with challenges, problems, and failures. There is no way to achievement and fulfillment by avoiding risk, problems, and failures. You cannot ever mimic or imitate anybody else because we are all unique with different strengths and weaknesses and view the world slightly different than the next.

Success isn't static. It's not about achieving your very next goal whether that is the technique of the day or winning the next competition. It's about perpetual progress and personal growth. You are either growing or dying. Once you achieve something, it's no longer as satisfying to you. If you learn a new move, it's exciting in the beginning as you refine and apply the technique on higher level competitors or training partners. But it doesn't last indefinitely. That's no different than life. You are no longer rejoicing graduating from high school from years ago. That was yesterday's big deal.

The things you are striving for in jiu-jitsu or in life is more akin to being bait. It's there to lure you into forward progress and personal development keeping you on a forward path of progress. Struggling to make forward progress causes you to evolve and adapt to changing conditions around you. But it is that same struggle that ends up delivering you the rewards, satisfaction, and personal fulfillment that leads to a successful life.

As we come to an end, it's fitting to close with the insights of Rilion Gracie. Rilion is the youngest son (one of 21 children) of the Grand Master Carlos Gracie, Sr. Born in Rio de Janeiro in 1963, Rilion grew up on the mats with his brothers and cousins. He is the nephew of Helio and younger brother of Rolls. Today he is one of the very few Coral Belts in existence globally (a 7th degree black belt) and has always believed that jiu-jitsu is for your entire life and not just as a hobby while you are young and strong.

He is a living testimonial of healthy living and using jiu-jitsu to improve life skills through the philosophical concepts of the martial art. Rilion is a man of principles, a believer of respect, hierarchy, discipline, self-control, self-confidence, and patience. He is also considered the most technical jiu-jitsu practitioner in the Gracie family and is known for always being "100% technical."

The stories of Rilion's technical skills are legendary. Growing up with some of the world's toughest brothers, uncles, and cousins, he trained with the greatest the sport had to offer in Brazil. It is said from those closest to him that he was never submitted as a black belt in competition or while training during his competitive career. His fundamentals and core essentials of jiu-jitsu are of such high caliber that it's next to impossible to submit him.

But jiu-jitsu is more than just a competitive outlet or as a world-class career instructor for Rilion. Jiu-jitsu is life and is to be done for life. As Rilion would explain, "The most important thing in life is the search for true essence, spiritual development to overcome life's difficulties, and to contribute to a better world for all of us. There is no doubt that jiu-jitsu when practiced and taught with its true principles, brings about physical, mental, and spiritual benefits."

When you pursue mastery of jiu-jitsu, you will be pursuing mastery of yourself. May you master your own life before you leave this life. Don't just strive to become a black belt in jiu-jitsu. Strive to become a black belt in life which includes your health, your finances, your career, your parenting, your relationships, and most importantly your self-awareness. And remember, in words repeated by Paulo Ribeiro, "Jiu-jitsu exists to make you quit." Jiu-jitsu is like most things in life. They exist to make you quit. But mastering yourself is all about not-quitting. Whatever you do in life, don't quit the hard things that are the most important to you.

For now, master jiu-jitsu, master life.

If you enjoyed this book, we would welcome a review on Amazon.com.

Index

Recommended For Further Reading

1. Brown, Peter & Roediger III, Henry & McDaniel, Mark (2014) *Make It Stick – The Science of Successful Learning,* Belknap Press: An Imprint of Harvard University Press
2. Dweck Ph.D., Carol S. (2006) *Mindset: The New Psychology of Success,* Random House, LLC
3. Larreche, J.C. (2008) *The Momentum Effect: How to Ignite Exceptional Growth,* FT Press
4. Long, Weldon (2013) *The Power of Consistency: Prosperity Mindset Training for Sales and Business Professionals,* Wiley
5. Willink, Jocko (2017) *Discipline Equals Freedom: Field Manual,* St. Martin's Press
6. Dalio, Ray (2017) *Principles: Life and Work,* Simon & Schuster
7. Keller, Gary & Papasan, Jay (2013) *The One Thing: The Surprisingly Simple Truth Behind Extraordinary Results,* Bard Press
8. Pressfield, Steven (2014) *Do The Work,* The Domino Project/Black Irish Entertainment
9. Waitzkin, Josh (2007) *The Art of Learning: An Inner Journey to Optimal Performance,* Free Press
10. Stulberg, Brad & Magness, Steve (2017) *Peak Performance: Elevate Your Game, Avoid Burnout, and Thrive with the New Science of Success,* Random House, LLC

11. Bandler, Richard & Grinder, John (1982) *Reframing: Neuro-Linguistic Programming and the Transformation of Meaning*, Real People Press

12. Robbins, Tony (2008) *Unlimited Power: The New Science of Personal Achievement*, Free Press

13. Brown, Brene (2015) *Daring Greatly: How the Courage to Be Vulnerable Transforms the Way We Live, Love, Parent, and Lead*, Avery

14. Tracy, Brian (2010) *Goals!: How to Get Everything You Want – Faster Than You Ever Thought Possible*, Berrett-Koehler Publishers

15. Gonzales, D.C. (2013) *The Art of Mental Training – A Guide to Performance Excellence*, GonzoLane Media

16. Holiday, Ryan (2016) *Ego Is The Enemy*, Penguin Group

17. Doepker, Derek & Kramer, Marjorie (2014) *The Healthy Habit Revolution: The Step by Step Blueprint to Create Better Habits in 5 Minutes a Day*

18. Burchard, Brendon (2017) *High Performance Habits: How Extraordinary People Become That Way*, Hay House

19. Coyle, Daniel (2009) *The Talent Code: Greatness Isn't Born. It's Grown. Here's How*, Bantam/Random House

20. Sinek, Simon (2009) *Start With Why: How Great Leaders Inspire Everyone to Take Action*, Penguin Group

21. Duckworth, Angela (2016) *Grit: The Power of Passion and Perseverance*, Simon and Schuster

22. Brady, Tom (2017) *The TB12 Method: How to Achieve a Lifetime of Sustained Peak Performance*

References

Chapter 1 - Introduction

1. Greene, Robert (2012) *Mastery,* Viking
2. Danaher, John. [Eat Films] YouTube. *"John Danaher Interview Jiu-Jitsu vs. The World"* (March 15, 2016) - https://www.youtube.com/watch?v=e_ffCW4joaU
3. Musashi, Miyamoto (1645) *Go Rin No Sho/The Book of Five Rings.*

Chapter 2 - Mindset

1. Dweck, Carol S. Ph.D. (2006) – *Mindset: The New Psychology of Success,* Random House
2. Gaither, Matthew. *"Martial Arts and the Midget Twister: This is Cris Rodriguez"* Cage Zombies, (May 9, 2016) http://www.cagezombies.com/2016/05/09/martial-arts-and-the-midget-twister-this-is-cris-rodriguez/
3. Gracie PAC MMA. YouTube. *"Cris 'Midget Twister' Rodriguez Receives BJJ Black Belt from Rob Kahn"* (September 26, 2012) - https://www.youtube.com/watch?v=AGUbHgRJqM0
4. Biz Women Rock! Podcast 073: *"Rodriguez: Martial Artist Turned Successful Business Woman"* http://bizwomenrock.com/cris-rodriguez-martial-artist-turned-successful-business-woman/

Chapter 3 - Momentum

1. The Grappling Central Podcast. Episode 247. *"Karel 'SilverFox' Pravec."* (December 19, 2017)
2. BJJ Heroes. *"Craig Kukuk"* https://www.bjjheroes.com/bjj-fighters/craig-kukuk
3. Wyman, Patrick. *"One-On-One with Firas Zahabi – Part 1."* Sherdog, (November 28, 2014) - http://www.sherdog.com/news/articles/OneonOne-with-Firas-Zahabi-Part-1-77855
4. Wikipedia. *"Six Degrees of Separation"* - https://en.wikipedia.org/wiki/Six_degrees_of_separation
5. Tristar Gym. YouTube. *"How To Program Your Mind For Fitness – The Power of Creating Momentum – Firas Zahabi"* (October 10, 2015) - https://www.youtube.com/watch?v=Q8K7ifs2Db4
6. Kindzia, Paul. (2017) *"30 Days To Better Health The Easy-Peasy Way – A Guide to Creating Health Processes, Getting Results, and Transforming Your Life In 30 Days,"* Paul Kindzia, Inc.
7. Larreche, J.C. (2008) *The Momentum Effect: How to Ignite Exceptional Growth*, FT Press

Chapter 4 - Consistency

1. Eastern Europe BJJ. *"The Success Story Behind Shoyoroll Brand"* (April 3, 2013) - https://www.bjjee.com/articles/the-success-story-behind-shoyoroll-brand/
2. Wilson, Elizabeth. Entrepreneur. *"RVCA: A Brand Like No Other; Learn how surf/skate label RVCA scores big by crafting a brand based on lifestyle."* (February 24, 2009) - https://www.entrepreneur.com/article/200320
3. BallerStatus. *"A Look Into RVCA Founder Pat Tenore's Life, By His Son Joseph."* (July 28, 2015) -

https://www.ballerstatus.com/2015/07/28/a-look-into-rvca-founder-pat-tenores-life-by-his-son-joseph/

4. BJJ Heroes. *"Rafael Mendes"* - https://www.bjjheroes.com/bjj-fighters/rafael-mendes-bjj-fighter-wiki

5. Art of Jiu-Jitsu Academy. YouTube. *"Rafael Mendes: Road To 6X"* (June 3, 2016) - https://www.youtube.com/watch?time_continue=16&v=qrBc_hA5ASA

6. Long, Weldon (2013) *The Power of Consistency: Prosperity Mindset Training for Sales and Business Professionals*, Wiley

Chapter 5 - Discipline

1. BJJ Heroes. *"Jean Jacques Machado"* - https://www.bjjheroes.com/bjj-fighters/jean-jacques-machado-bjj-fighter-wiki

2. The Grumpy Grappler. *"Deconstructing the Gracie Mythology (Part 1)"* (Tuesday, June 3, 2014) - http://philosophycommons.typepad.com/the_grumpy_grappler/2014/06/deconstructing-the-gracie-mythology.html

3. The Grumpy Grappler. *"Deconstructing the Gracie Mythology (Part 2)"* (Tuesday, June 10, 2014) - http://philosophycommons.typepad.com/the_grumpy_grappler/2014/06/deconstructing-the-gracie-mythology-part-2.html

4. BJJ Heroes. *"Oswaldo Fadda"* - https://www.bjjheroes.com/bjj-fighters/oswaldo-fadda-facts-and-bio

5. Willink, Jocko (2017) *Discipline Equals Freedom: Field Manual*, St. Martin's Press

Chapter 6 - Principles

1. Dalio, Ray (2017) *Principles: Life and Work*, Simon & Schuster

2. Gracie Mag. *"15 Basic Jiu-Jitsu Principles For A Happier and Healthier Lifestyle"* (November 4, 2015) - http://www.graciemag.com/en/2015/11/04/15-basic-jiu-jitsu-principles-for-a-happier-and-healthier-lifestyle/

3. Canaria, Kitt. Jiu-Jitsu Times. *"The Top 3 Combat Principles Applied in Business."* (January 15, 2016) - https://www.jiujitsutimes.com/the-top-3-combat-principles-applied-in-business/

4. BJJ Heroes. *"Ryron Gracie."* - https://www.bjjheroes.com/bjj-fighters/ryron-gracie

5. GracieAcademy. YouTube. *"Gracie Philosophy: Powerful Principles and Egoless Sparring."* (June 3, 2010) - https://www.youtube.com/watch?v=xQT4GVYBCkE

6. allthingsbjj. YouTube. *"The Principles of Gracie Jiu-Jitsu with Rener Gracie."* (September 19, 2012) - https://www.youtube.com/watch?v=WSS7IYSs7WY

7. Djokovic, Iva. *"Rickson Influences HUGE Changes to Gracie University."* (June 7, 2016) - https://www.bjjee.com/articles/rickson-influences-huge-changes-to-gracie-university-2/

8. BJJ Heroes. *"Rickson Gracie"* - https://www.bjjheroes.com/bjj-fighters/rickson-gracie-facts-and-bio

Chapter 7 - Processes

1. Wikipedia. *"Paducah, Kentucky"* - https://en.wikipedia.org/wiki/Paducah,_Kentucky

2. Three Rivers Academy. *"About Us"* - http://threeriversacademy.com/about-us/

3. Facebook. *"Eli Knight"* - https://www.facebook.com/elirknight

4. Coloradofightsource. YouTube. *"Fight to Win Owner Seth Daniels pt 1."* (March 17, 2011) - https://www.youtube.com/watch?v=aKH7tKUVbdU

5. Coloradofightsource. YouTube. *"Fight to Win Owner Seth Daniels pt 2."* (March 17, 2011) - https://www.youtube.com/watch?v=UAAwh8YxaK8

6. Garcia, Raphael. SB Nation/Bloody Elbow. *"Fight to Win Pro Brings A New Look To Grappling."* (May 17, 2017) - https://www.bloodyelbow.com/2017/5/17/15647222/fight-to-win-pro-grappling-grappling-bjj-no-gi-concerts-tournaments-interview-jiu-jitsu

7. Clements, Averi. Jiu-Jitsu Times. *"F2W Pro CEO Seth Daniels Wins Fans' Hearts After Stepping In To Compete Last-Minute Just 48 Hours After Being Robbed."* (June 14, 2017) - https://www.jiujitsutimes.com/beyonseth-fight-to-win-pro/

8. Clements, Averi. FloGrappling. *"Fight To Win Pro Is On Track To Pay Athletes $1 Million By The End Of 2017."* (February 23, 2017) - https://www.flograppling.com/articles/5061683-fight-to-win-pro-is-on-track-to-pay-athletes-1-million-by-the-end-of-2017

9. BJJ Heroes. *"Rubens Charles "Cobrinha."* - https://www.bjjheroes.com/bjj-fighters/rubens-charles-cobrinha-bjj-fighter-wiki

10. BamaPride RollTide. YouTube. *"The Perfectionist."* (November 4, 2013) - https://www.youtube.com/watch?v=VwSaS9geI1U

11. Page, Susan. (2015) *"The Power of Business Process Improvement: 10 Simple Steps to Increase Effectiveness, Efficiency, and Adaptability."* Amacom Publishing.

Chapter 8 - Adaptability

1. BJJ Heroes. *"BJ Penn"* - https://www.bjjheroes.com/bjj-fighters/bj-penn-wiki

2. BJJ Heroes. *"Keenan Cornelius"* - https://www.bjjheroes.com/bjj-fighters/keenan-cornelius

3. BJJ Heroes. *"Andre Galvao"* - https://www.bjjheroes.com/bjj-fighters/andre-galvao-bjj-and-mma-fighter-wiki

4. Canfield, Jack. (2015) *"The Success Principles: How To Get From Where You Are To Where You Want To Be."* William Morrow Paperbacks

5. Ericsson, Anders & Pool, Robert. (2017) *"Peak: Secrets From The New Science Of Expertise."* Eamon Dolan/Mariner Books

6. Strenuous Life Podcast (GrappleArts). Episode 14. *"Keenan Cornelius on Training, BJJ Competition, MMA Goals and More"* (April 24, 2013) - https://www.grapplearts.com/keenan-cornelius-on-training-bjj-competition-mma-goals-and-more/

7. The Grappling Central Podcast. Episode 7. *"Andre Galvao."* (March 31, 2016)

8. The Grappling Central Podcast. Episode 120. *"Andre Galvao Returns."* (September 29, 2016)

Chapter 9 – Minimize and Simplify

1. BJJ Heroes. *"Bernardo Faria"* - https://www.bjjheroes.com/bjj-fighters/bernardo-faria-facts-and-bio

2. Wikipedia. *"Favela"* - https://en.wikipedia.org/wiki/Favela

3. Wikipedia. *"Maslow's Hierarchy of Needs"* - https://en.wikipedia.org/wiki/Maslow%27s_hierarchy_of_needs

4. BJJ Heroes. *"Roger Gracie"* - https://www.bjjheroes.com/bjj-fighters/roger-gracie-bio

5. Keller, Gary & Papasan, Jay (2013) *The One Thing: The Surprisingly Simple Truth Behind Extraordinary Results*, Bard Press

6. Strenuous Life Podcast (GrappleArts). Episode 28. *"How Bernardo Faria Won Double Gold at the BJJ Mundials."* (July 5, 2015) - https://www.grapplearts.com/how-bernardo-faria-won-double-gold-at-the-bjj-mundials/

7. Strenuous Life Podcast (GrappleArts). Episode 86. *"BJJ World Champion Bernardo Faria On Surviving Adversity Kidnapping."* (September 27, 2017) - https://www.grapplearts.com/strenuous-life-podcast-bernardo-faria/

8. Strenuous Life Podcast (GrappleArts). Episode 43. *"Training and Competition Strategies of Bernardo Faria."* (February 3, 2017) - https://www.grapplearts.com/training-competition-strategies-bernardo-faria/

9. The Grappling Central Podcast. Episode 10. *"Bernardo Faria."* (March 31, 2016)

10. The Grappling Central Podcast. Episode 77. *"Roger Gracie."* (May 6, 2016)

11. The Grappling Central Podcast. Episode 235. *"Roger Gracie Returns!."* (November 7, 2017)

Chapter 10 – Tracking and Benchmarking

1. Collins, Jim (2001) *"From Good To Great: Why Some Companies Make the Leap…and Others Don't"* Harper Business

2. Pressfield, Steven (2014) *Do The Work*, The Domino

3. The Grappling Central Podcast. Episode 45. *"Jason Scully."* (January 15, 2016)

Chapter 11 – Deep Learning

1. BJJ Heroes. *"Leandro Lo"* - https://www.bjjheroes.com/bjj-fighters/leandro-lo-pereira
2. Dweck, Carol S. Ph.D. (2006) – *"Mindset: The New Psychology of Success,"* Random House
3. Coyle, Daniel (2009) *"The Talent Code: Greatness Isn't Born. It's Grown. Here's How,"* Bantam/Random House
4. Teagu, Hywel. FloGrappling. *"From ADCC To SUG: Breakout Star Craig Jones' Roller-Coaster Week."* (October 4, 2017) - https://www.flograppling.com/articles/6014613-from-adcc-to-sug-breakout-star-craig-jones-roller-coaster-week
5. ADCC Submission Fighting World Federation. *"ADCC Worlds 2017 Complete Results and Brackets."* (September 24, 2017) - http://adcombat.com/adcc-worlds-2017-complete-results-and-brackets/
6. FloGrappling. *"Leandro Lo vs. Craig Jones ADCC 2017 World Championships."* (September 23, 2017) - https://www.flograppling.com/video/6012358-leandro-lo-vs-craig-jones-adcc-2017-world-championships
7. BJJ Scandinavia. *"Watch Craig Jones and Kit Dale Sparring With Hilarious Commentary."* (October 1, 2017) - http://www.bjjscandinavia.com/2017/10/01/watch-craig-jones-kit-dale-sparring-hilarious-commentary/
8. Sperlazza, Courtney. BulletProof Blog. *"What You Need To Know About Myelin and The Top 12 Ways To Support Your Brain."* (September 22, 2017) - https://blog.bulletproof.com/need-know-myelin-top-12-ways-support-brain/
9. Waitzkin, Josh (2007) *The Art of Learning: An Inner Journey to Optimal Performance,* Free Press

Chapter 12 – Workload and Stress

1. Stulberg, Brad & Magness, Steve (2017) *Peak Performance: Elevate Your Game, Avoid Burnout, and Thrive with the New Science of Success*, Random House, LLC

2. Higdon, Hal. Training Peaks. *"Losing and Regaining Fitness."* (March 28, 2018) - https://www.trainingpeaks.com/blog/losing-and-regaining-fitness/

3. Strenuous Life Podcast (GrappleArts). Episode 34. *"Rob Biernacki on The Underlying Principles of Brazilian Jiu-Jitsu."* (March 29, 2016)

4. Strenuous Life Podcast (GrappleArts). Episode 36. *"BJJ Q&A with Rob Biernacki"* (September 28, 2016)

5. Strenuous Life Podcast (GrappleArts). Episode 82. *"A BJJ School Where Visiting Schools Can Train For Free?"* (September 9, 2017)

6. Strenuous Life Podcast (GrappleArts). Episode 110. *"Training With World Champions, with Rob Biernacki"* (January 17, 2018)

7. Strenuous Life Podcast (GrappleArts). Episode 116. *"Should You Pull Guard in BJJ Competition or Not"* (February 12, 2018)

Chapter 13 - Modeling

1. BJJ Heroes. *"Marcelo Garcia"* - https://www.bjjheroes.com/bjj-fighters/marcelo-garcia-fighter-profile

2. Dailymotion. *"Marcelo Garcia v. Ricco Rodriguez."* (April 3, 2007) - https://www.dailymotion.com/video/x1mbho

3. Live Your Legend. *"On Modeling the Impossible and How to Do Anything."* (January 25, 2014) - https://liveyourlegend.net/on-modeling-the-impossible-and-how-to-do-anything/

4. The Tim Ferriss Experiment. *"Brazilian Jiu-Jitsu. Episode 8. Tim heads to New York City to get his ass kicked by the "Michael Jordan of jiu-jitsu, world champion Marcelo Garcia."* (April 27,

2015) - https://itunes.apple.com/us/tv-season/the-tim-ferriss-experiment/id984734983

5. Bandler, Richard & Grinder, John (1982) *Reframing: Neuro-Linguistic Programming and the Transformation of Meaning*, Real People Press

6. Robbins, Tony (2008) *Unlimited Power: The New Science of Personal Achievement*, Free Press

7. Waitzkin, Josh (2007) *The Art of Learning: An Inner Journey to Optimal Performance*, Free Press

8. The Grappling Central Podcast. Episode 207. *"Marcelo Garcia."* (August 1, 2017)

Chapter 14 – Do Your Best

1. Wikipedia. *"Sorbonne."* - https://en.wikipedia.org/wiki/Sorbonne

2. Wikipedia. *"Citizenship in a Republic"* - https://en.wikipedia.org/wiki/Citizenship_in_a_Republic

3. Eastern Europe BJJ. *"US President Teddy Roosevelt Trained Jiu-Jitsu & Judo."* (August 13, 2015) - https://www.bjjee.com/articles/us-president-teddy-roosevelt-trained-jiu-jitsu-judo/

4. Zahar, Chris. Jiu-Jitsu Times. *"Who is Tom Davey?"* (July 6, 2017) - https://www.jiujitsutimes.com/who-is-tom-davey/

5. Albin, Nick. ChewJitsu. *"Make BJJ Competitions Fun By Focusing On Yourself."* (June 17, 2018) - http://www.chewjitsu.net/category/inspiration/

6. Brown, Brene (2015) *Daring Greatly: How the Courage to Be Vulnerable Transforms the Way We Live, Love, Parent, and Lead*, Avery

7. Strenuous Life Podcast (GrappleArts). Episode 120. *"Nick 'Chewy' Albin from Chewjitsu on BJJ, Wrestling, MMA and More."* (February 23, 2018)

Chapter 15 - Goals

1. BJJ Heroes. *"Yuri Simoes"* - https://www.bjjheroes.com/bjj-fighters/yuri-simoes

2. Clements, Averi. FloGrappling. *"Judo Olympian Travis Stevens To Face ADCC Champ In Sub-Only Jiu-Jitsu."* (July 24, 2017) - https://www.flograppling.com/articles/5068501-judo-olympian-travis-stevens-to-face-adcc-champ-in-sub-only-jiu-jitsu

3. JudoCrazy. *"Q&A with Travis Stevens."* (September 12, 2017) - http://www.judocrazy.com/2017/09/q-with-travis-stevens.html

4. Stevens, Travis. YouTube. *"John Danaher talk Philosophy of BJJ and about Travis Stevens."* (March 8, 2016) - https://www.youtube.com/watch?time_continue=164&v=KbhXppC0pTE

5. Eastern Europe BJJ. *"How Travis Stevens Overcomes Injuries With His Mind."* (December 2, 2017) - https://www.bjjee.com/articles/travis-stevens-overcomes-injuries-mind/

6. Zenga, Michael. BJJ Fanatics. *"What I've Learned Filming The Best Guys In The World: 3 Common Themes by Michael Zenga."* - https://bjjfanatics.com/blogs/news/what-i-ve-learned-filming-the-best-guys-in-the-world-3-common-themes-by-michael-zenga

7. BJJ Fanatics. *"How Are Those 2018 Resolutions Coming?"* - https://bjjfanatics.com/blogs/news/how-are-those-2018-resolutions-coming

8. BJJ Fanatics. *"How Social Media Can Ensure You Reach Your Health Goals."* - https://bjjfanatics.com/blogs/news/how-social-media-can-ensure-you-reach-your-health-goals

9. BJJ Fanatics. *"The Evolution of Your BJJ Goals."* - https://bjjfanatics.com/blogs/news/the-evolution-of-your-bjj-goals

10. Tracy, Brian (2010) *Goals!: How to Get Everything You Want – Faster Than You Ever Thought Possible*, Berrett-Koehler Publishers

11. Strenuous Life Podcast (GrappleArts). Episode 96. *"Lessons Learned from 19 Different World Champions, with Mike Zenga."* (November 9, 2017)

Chapter 16 - Visualization

1. Gonzales, D.C. (2013) *The Art of Mental Training – A Guide to Performance Excellence*, GonzoLane Media

2. BJJ Heroes. *"Livia Gluchowska"* - https://www.bjjheroes.com/bjj-fighters/livia-gluchowska

3. BJJ Heroes. *"Mackenzie Dern"* - https://www.bjjheroes.com/bjj-fighters/mackenzie-dern

Chapter 17 - Ego

1. Mooney, Michael. Success. *"The Jocko Willink Way."* (March 13, 2017) - https://www.success.com/the-jocko-willink-way/

2. Teague, Hywel. BJJ Hacks TV. YouTube. *"Braulio Estima: Dealing with Ego in Jiu-Jitsu."* (June 3, 2013) - https://www.youtube.com/watch?v=muaOXUD5r5Y

3. Djokovic, Iva. Eastern Europe BJJ. *"Jiu-Jitsu: A Game of Ego."* (May 7, 2017) - https://www.bjjee.com/articles/jiu-jitsu-game-ego/

4. DeBlass, Tom. Facebook. *"Stop Being Afraid to Look Bad in The Training Room."* (May 3, 2017) - https://www.facebook.com/photo.php?fbid=10158587351955627&set=a.10150693394045627.704197.654680626&type=3&theater

5. Holiday, Ryan (2016) *Ego Is The Enemy*, Penguin Group
6. The Grappling Central Podcast. Episode 65. *"Tom DeBlass."* (March 22, 2016)
7. The Grappling Central Podcast. Episode 151. *"Tom DeBlass is Back!."* (January 17, 2017)
8. The Grappling Central Podcast. Episode 217. *"Tom DeBlass Returns."* (September 5, 2017)

Chapter 18 - Habit

1. Octagon News. YouTube. *"Joe Rogan – This Is My Daily Routine."* (June 22, 2017) - https://www.youtube.com/watch?v=14rvts7tptw
2. Wikipedia. *"Matt Arroyo"* - https://en.wikipedia.org/wiki/Matt_Arroyo
3. Doepker, Derek & Kramer, Marjorie (2014) *The Healthy Habit Revolution: The Step by Step Blueprint to Create Better Habits in 5 Minutes a Day*
4. Burchard, Brendon (2017) *High Performance Habits: How Extraordinary People Become That Way*, Hay House
5. The Grappling Central Podcast. Episode 79. *"Matt Arroyo."* (May 12, 2016)

Chapter 19 - Art

1. Mullen, Mark. Jiu-Jitsu Times. *"Evolve's New Coach, Stuart Cooper, Captures The World Of BJJ On Film."* (January 14, 2017) - https://www.jiujitsutimes.com/evolves-new-coach-stuart-cooper-captures-world-bjj-film/
2. Tiger Muay Thai & Mixed Martial Arts. *"Where In The World Is Stuart Cooper?"* (May 2, 2014) - https://www.tigermuaythai.com/where-in-the-world-is-stuart-cooper

3. Tiger Muay Thai and MMA Training Camp, Phuket,
    Thailand. YouTube. *"Where In The World Is Stuart Cooper?"*
    (May 2, 2014) -
    https://www.youtube.com/watch?v=v_F67lviKZI&feature=
    youtu.be
4. BJJ Heroes. *"Eddie Bravo"* - https://www.bjjheroes.com/bjj-
    fighters/eddie-bravo
5. Wikipedia. *"Eddie Bravo."* -
    https://en.wikipedia.org/wiki/Eddie_Bravo
6. Submissions101. YouTube. *"Eddie Bravo vs Royler Gracie
    (entire match) ADCC 2003."* (June 15, 2008) -
    https://www.youtube.com/watch?v=Y4ASonA9t6c
7. ConvertKit. YouTube. *"Your Job Is To Make Art: Why We Need
    Generosity More Than Ever – Seth Godin at Craft & Commerce
    2017"* (December 13, 2017) -
    https://www.youtube.com/watch?v=rdUeq09cGJ0&feature=
    youtu.be&ck_subscriber_id=89859203
8. The Grappling Central Podcast. Episode 27. *"Eddie Bravo."*
    (November 15, 2015)

Chapter 20 – Personal Growth

1. BJJ Heroes. *"Eddie Cummings."* -
    https://www.bjjheroes.com/bjj-fighters/eddie-cummings
2. Djokovic, Iva. Eastern Europe BJJ. *"John Danaher Explains Why
    Eddie Cummings and Jonathan Calestine No Longer Take His
    Classes."* (February 19, 2018) -
    https://www.bjjee.com/articles/john-danaher-explains-
    eddie-cummings-jonathan-calestine-no-longer-take-classes/
3. Clements, Averi. FloGrappling. *"Jiu-Jitsu's Einstein: Inside The
    Mind of Eddie Cummings."* (September 12, 2017) -
    https://www.flograppling.com/articles/6006631-jiu-jitsus-
    einstein-inside-the-mind-of-eddie-cummings

4. BJJ Heroes. *"John Danaher"* - https://www.bjjheroes.com/bjj-fighters/john-danaher

5. BJJ Fanatics. *"John Danaher – Leglocks: Enter The System"* - https://bjjfanatics.com/pages/enter-the-system-by-john-danaher

6. Coyle, Daniel (2009) *The Talent Code: Greatness Isn't Born. It's Grown. Here's How*, Bantam/Random House

7. Tracy, Brian. YouTube. *"No Limits: Change Your Life With Personal Growth."* (March 1, 2013) - https://www.youtube.com/watch?v=SGK2rRcsTHo

8. Strenuous Life Podcast (GrappleArts). Episode 33. *"Eddie 'Wolverine' Cummings on Leglocks, Leglocks, Leglocks"* (February 24, 2016)

Chapter 21 - Why

1. Graugart, Christian. (2012) *"The Brazilian Jiu-Jitsu Globetrotter: The True Story About A Frantic, 140 Day Long, Around-The-World Trip To Train Brazilian Jiu-Jitsu."* CreateSpace Independent Publishing

2. Sinek, Simon. TED Ideas Worth Spreading. *"How Great Leaders Inspire Action."* (September 2009) - https://www.ted.com/talks/simon_sinek_how_great_leaders_inspire_action

3. Sinek, Simon (2009) *Start With Why: How Great Leaders Inspire Everyone to Take Action*, Penguin Group

4. BJJ Heroes. *"Renzo Gracie"* - https://www.bjjheroes.com/bjj-fighters/renzo-gracie-bjj-fighter

5. Wikipedia. *"Gracie Family"* - https://en.wikipedia.org/wiki/Gracie_family

6. The Grappling Central Podcast. Episode 71. *"Renzo Gracie."* (April 14, 2016)

Chapter 22 - Perseverance

1. Paulo Ribeiro Brazilian Jiu-Jitsu. *"Instructors."* - http://prbjjnaples.com/Instructors/Paulo-Ribeiro

2. Duckworth, Angela (2016) *Grit: The Power of Passion and Perseverance*, Simon and Schuster

3. Scelfo, Julie. New York Times. *"Angela Duckworth on Passion, Grit and Success."* (April 8, 2016) - https://www.nytimes.com/2016/04/10/education/edlife/passion-grit-success.html

4. Bidwell, Mike. Jiu-Jitsu Times. *"Mike Bidwell."* - https://www.jiujitsutimes.com/author/mikebidwell/

5. Mullen, Mark. Jiu-Jitsu Times. *"Off The Mat With A BJJ Black Belt: Mike 'The Spider-Ninja' Bidwell."* (April 14, 2016) - https://www.jiujitsutimes.com/off-mat-bjj-black-belt-mike-spider-ninja-bidwell/

6. Mullen, Mark. Jiu-Jitsu Times. *"Mike Bidwell On Being A Brown Belt For 13 Years."* (April 17, 2016) - https://www.jiujitsutimes.com/mike-bidwell-brown-belt-13-years/

7. Eastern Europe BJJ. *"13 Years A Brown Belt: The Incredible Journey of Mike Bidwell."* (August 21, 2015) - https://www.bjjee.com/videos/13-years-a-brown-belt-the-incredible-journey-of-mike-bidwell/

8. Ezine Articles. *"About Stephen Whittier"* (January 28, 2013) - https://ezinearticles.com/expert/Stephen_Whittier/1490585

9. Whittier International. *"Home"* - https://stephenwhittier.com/home12121646

10. Strenuous Life Podcast (GrappleArts). Episode 26. *"Steve Whittier on SBG's Drills for BJJ Excellence."* (March 24, 2015)

Chapter 23 - Longevity

1. Brady, Tom (2017) *The TB12 Method: How to Achieve a Lifetime of Sustained Peak Performance*

2. BJJ Heroes. *"Alexandre Xande Ribeiro"* - https://www.bjjheroes.com/bjj-fighters/xande-ribeiro-fighter-wiki

3. BJJ Heroes. *"Saulo Ribeiro"* - https://www.bjjheroes.com/bjj-fighters/saulo-ribeiro-facts-and-bio

4. Ribeiro, Saulo & Howell, Kevin. (2008) *"Jiu-Jitsu University"* Victory Belt Publishing

5. Costa, Diogo. YouTube. "Xande Ribeiro – *'The Amazon Warrior' – Jiu-Jitsu Highlights (2015)"* (June 24, 2015) - https://www.youtube.com/watch?v=xhXP4Yr70Pc

6. Trindade, Ivan. Jiu-Jitsu Magazine. *"Exclusive: Xande Shares His Secrets For Staying On Top Of The Game For More Than 15 Years."* (September 7, 2016) - http://jiujitsumag.com/exclusive-xande-shares-his-secrets-for-staying-on-top-of-the-game-for-more-than-15-years/

7. The Grappling Central Podcast. Episode 52. *"Xande Ribeiro."* (February 11, 2016)

Chapter 24 - Conclusion

1. Dalio, Ray. Principles. *"Principles For Success: An Ultra Mini-Series Adventure."* - https://www.principles.com/principles-for-success/#play

2. Rilion Gracie Headquarters. *"Rilion Gracie"* - http://riliongracie.com/rilion-gracie/

3. BJJ Heroes. *"Rilion Gracie"* - https://www.bjjheroes.com/bjj-fighters/rilion-gracie

The Author

Paul Kindzia is a writer, health and wellness advocate, entrepreneur, wealth advisor, and CEO of Kindzia Investments, Inc. a registered investment advisory practice outside of Atlanta, GA. His personal mission is to teach others how to improve their health and wealth and improve their happiness.

Paul is a certified public accountant with an undergraduate degree from the State University of New York at Buffalo (1992). He also holds an MBA in corporate finance from the State University of New York at Buffalo (1994). He is a member of the American Institute of Certified Public Accountants.

Paul is a Certified Financial Planner (CFP®).

He is an avid reader and writer with an ever-expanding personal library. He has a love of nature, science, animals, and the ocean.

Paul is a proponent of maintaining personal health and wellness. He enjoys an active and healthy lifestyle and is a 13-time Ironman triathlon finisher. He has also completed numerous marathons including but not limited to the San Diego Rock N' Roll Marathon, Nashville Country Music Marathon,

Disney Marathon, New York City Marathon, and his personal favorite the Marine Corp Marathon in Washington, D.C.

Paul lives outside of Atlanta, GA with his family and an ever-expanding pack of rescue dogs. He is an animal lover at heart and the family often volunteers with English Springer Rescue America (ESRA) or helping some stray cats.

He also enjoys behavioral finance, investments, endurance athletics, martial arts, music, video production, making sushi and has a tremendous passion for fishing, and scuba diving.

He is officially a jiu-jitsu junkie.

You can keep up with him at www.paulkindzia.com **and** www.masterjiujitsumasterlife.com

For additional valuable information including free resources, please visit our website at:

www.paulkindzia.com

www.masterjiujitsumasterlife.com

Be sure to check out our other publications

Printed in Great Britain
by Amazon

80215561R00174